Don't Take It Lying Down
Life According to the Goddess

DR KAALII CARGILL

ISBN-13: 978-1482721959

ISBN-10: 1482721953

Cover art by the author
Cover image Copyright © 2002 Erica Lewis

This book is for you.
For all women.
For the grandmothers.
And the granddaughters who will inherit the
myths by which we live.

ADAM, EVE AND LILITH, IN THE GARDEN OF EDEN[1]

CONTENTS

Acknowledgments

To fully acknowledge those who have supported me in writing this book, I found myself going back again to the beginning. Behind me is an unbroken line of mothers and daughters as old as time. My mother, Lorna May Goldsworthy, gifted me with a love of reading and writing and a healthy disrespect for convention. My grandmothers, Gladys and Carmella, with dolls and oranges, will and determination, stories, songs, and dark archaic eyes of power are a part of me and of this work. No less the fathers and grandfathers. My father, Antonio Taverna taught a small girl to negotiate stairs and to see the light in Nature, and grandfather Reg patiently sponsored learning and curiosity. The family lines continue with Aram, Saascha, Qi, and Charni, and their children, Jessi, Joshua, Jade, Ruben, Sonny, Harry, Willow, and the rest waiting to be born. The richness of my journey with the feminine mysteries began in the ground of mother and I have been amply blessed by the depth of relationship with my family.

There are so many relatives, friends, colleagues, and fellow journeyers who have also offered support: Beornn, Deidre, Derek, Esther, James, Jascha, Karin, Lindy, Lisa, Lucca, Lihla, Paul, Peter, Posy, Robyn, Simon, and Stephen. Thank you to Rena and Helen for the years of ritual and magic, Rachana for the eagles, Anita, Carol, Charni, Deidre, Irene, Mary, Philomena, Saascha, and Sandra for carefully reading early drafts of the manuscript, David for the photographs and other ways of seeing, and Erica for the cover image.

One of the central facts of my life for the last 38 years has been my husband, Andrew, whose authentic seeking has taken me on a remarkable journey. Our shared vision in working with psyche provides the temenos from which I work.

I am grateful to so many teachers, from those early on who opened doors and took me out into Nature and taught me to value my differences, to those more recently: Philip Greenway, who supervised my PhD so that I knew it was truly mine, and Peter O"Connor, who bestowed blessings. And all the wise women who have offered inspiration and encouragement, including Robbie Davis-Floyd, Riane Eisler, and Normandi Ellis.

I especially thank all the women who have shared their stories about birth control and participated so fully in the early stages of bringing this book to life: Angela, Anita, Anne, Barbara, Carol, Catherine, Christine, Dot, Elspeth, Fran, Frances, Irene, Jan, Jenni, Joanne, Judy, Katharine, Kushna, Maria, Marion, Michelle, Natalie, Nicole, Nicky, Rhea, Robyn, Rose, Ruth, Sallyanne, Sandra, Sunderai, Tracy, Yasmin.

At the beginning and always there is Lilith, guide to the mysteries.

KAALII CARGILL

INTRODUCTION

This book will change your life.

It invites you to see through the collective beliefs, attitudes and practices that bind women to a world view that denies power, choice, and control in so many aspects of our lives. It is about the feminine principle and what has been lost. It is about reclaiming our birthright.

This is also a book about mindbody birth control. This radical approach challenges many of our culture's assumptions about women and power. You can take up mindbody birth control as a practice, or you can use it as inspiration for what becomes possible when we don't take it lying down.

When we discover what it is to be truly feminine, we reconnect with the experience of God as a woman--the Goddess in all her names. And when we invite the Goddess back in to our lives, *She changes everything She touches and everything She touches changes.*

The stories and sacred tasks in this book are keys that open doors to ancient mysteries that once guided women through their lives. The Goddess waits patiently for us to come to her, and we must each travel our own journey to the deep feminine wisdom that is every woman's birthright.

Let's start at the very beginning . . .

Hebrew myth tells the story of Adam's first wife, Lilith, who was also created from earth. When Lilith refused to assume the missionary position, Adam tried to force her. Lilith uttered the name of God and left the Garden. Some say that she returned in the form of the serpent and offered Eve the apple. The rest is his-story. This book offers another bite of that apple by telling part of her-story, Lilith's story, the story of women's mysteries lost and found . . .

I invite you to embark on a journey that will challenge much of what you have been taught as truth. You will come to understand just how relative to time and place our current version of truth is. Things are not what they seem. What happens if we don't take it lying down?

These pages weave a tapestry of ancient women's mysteries lost and found. You can engage sacred practices that open the way to connecting with the intrinsic power of the feminine to manage fertility and the rest of life in a very different way.

I have included information from women's spirituality, psychobiology, Jungian psychology, mythology, and anthropology to describe and explain the possibilities that emerge when we see through our conditioning. There are also the personal stories of the many women I have interviewed, a reminder that this book is fundamentally about women's stories, women's lives. About your story, your life.

I also tell stories from my life . . .

In the drought years of 2003/4 in South eastern Australia, water restrictions were introduced. We were unable to water our lawns. My lawn at the time was a strip in front of the house along the footpath, the "Nature strip" of suburban life. From my second story bathroom I rigged up a hose that siphoned my bath water onto the lawn. It was the greenest strip in the street.

Siphoning water is a simple process. With the top end of the hose in the bath, I attached the bottom end of the hose to the tap for a few seconds so that water flowed back up the hose. Then I disconnected the hose from the tap, and the water ran out, creating suction to draw out the bath water. One night I had left the bath water ready for siphoning in the morning, but when I woke the bath had emptied itself. At first I was mystified; how had the water siphoned itself out of the bath? Then I discovered that I had moved the bottom end of the hose to a lower garden bed the previous night. The small drop in height was enough to set off the siphoning process.

Water running downhill is a force of Nature. Given the slightest encouragement, it will flow. The Goddess, the feminine archetype, is also a force of Nature. Given the slightest encouragement, the waters of Her living womb will flow through our lives.

In the modern world, however, we seldom encounter the Goddess as a force of Nature. If we are fortunate, She touches us through our sexuality and our experiences with fertility: menstruation, conception, pregnancy, childbirth, nurturing. Yet these areas of life have become increasingly modernized, managed, and degraded; the forces of Nature have been dimmed. The waters no longer flow as they once did.

And yet there is trickle here and there, a suspicious dampness in our eyes or in our sex, a memory of bathing in the waters of Her living womb.

One of the strongest links we still have to the Goddess is through the life-giving power of the feminine. Women still give life through their bodies. This is so obvious that we forget the magic of it. Life does not come through men's bodies, test tubes, or incubators; life still comes into being through women's bodies. Despite contraceptive chemicals and more than two thousand years of negative conditioning, women's bodies continue to respond to the cycles of the moon, to the rhythms of Nature. The ancient magic of the life-giving power of the feminine is still with us.

Take a moment to consider the extraordinary fact that women have always been able to do something that men cannot do: grow and bring forth new life from their bodies. That we take this for granted (and even see it as a burden women must bear) represents a terrible loss of power. Women are the life-givers, and this is a sacred task.

Today we are on the threshold of losing this. To science and technology. To the misinformation of a patriarchal culture that denigrates Nature. To our own complacency. We are facing one of the greatest threats since the takeover of women's ways two or three thousand years ago.

This book explores themes of fertility and birth control, power and choice, that have their roots in ancient feminine mysteries and traditions. You will discover a tapestry of historical events, mythological, philosophical and psychological understandings that raise challenging questions about conventional thinking. Are you ready for a journey of discovery and reconnection with your deep inner wisdom? Are you ready to reclaim your birthright as a daughter in the unbroken line of mothers and daughters that goes back to the Goddess?

I have written this book as a guide to a process that I hope you can take up and make your own in the ways that work for you. It may not be directly about birth control for you; the information in this book applies to all aspects of life.

If you are interested in mindbody birth control, it is important for you to know that the whole practice is not just about mind over matter. It is a process of immersion in the relationship between mind and body, psyche and matter, a relationship that has taken many twists and turns since the beginning of time. The bigger story of what has happened to women's mysteries throughout the ages is a vital part of this work.

We are at the threshold of another revolution and have an opportunity to participate in what may be a crucial turning for the continuance of life on Earth. How each of us approaches this relationship will impact on the Earth, the original matter . . . mater . . . mother of us all.

PART I

THE LIFE-GIVING POWER OF THE FEMININE

CHAPTER ONE

ANCIENT WISDOM LOST AND FOUND

Once upon a time, when "God was a woman"[2], anywhere from 35000 years ago until about 3500 years ago in some parts of the world, the life-giving power of the Goddess was deeply respected. Consistent with this, women were respected as the life-givers, and the functions of pregnancy, birth, and nurturing were valued as reflections of the Great Mother, the mother of all. The rhythms and cycles of Nature were honoured in ceremonies and rituals, in daily practices that reflected a reverence for the feminine principle.

Over the last few thousand years, this has changed so that the world in which we now live has little of this respect and acknowledgement. These changes have resulted in the loss of ancient ways of knowing.

Women in some parts of the world did once know how to manage fertility in a simple, uncomplicated internal way, with little need to use any outside devices or programs. If these were needed, there is considerable evidence that simple, safe birth control was also available in the form of vaginal sponges, herbs and abortifacient drugs. [3]

This is a very different story from the official version of history which tells us that women were at the mercy of Nature during their childbearing years until the advent of the contraceptive Pill.

This other story tells of women's mysteries destroyed by church and state authorities and various individuals, all of whom were jealous and/or fearful of women's life-giving power. In this story (herstory rather than history), there are social, religious and cultural factors that have deeply affected the way we think about ourselves, our bodies, and the relationship between psyche and matter. These factors have profoundly impacted on fertility management, resulting in our loss of true reproductive autonomy.

Even more tragically, there is also amnesia for our true past. There are things that have been forgotten which should not have been forgotten. In the following chapters, I tell the story of this forgetting so that you can begin the process of remembering (gathering the dismembered parts and making them whole).

In the ancient Egyptian mystery tradition, there is a story of dismemberment in which the scattered parts are then re-membered or gathered up. The God-King, Osiris, was the principle of generativity and growth, the original Green Man of Nature. His brother, Seth, represented the principle of limitation. Consumed with jealousy for his popular brother, Seth cut Osiris into 14 pieces and scattered the dismembered parts far and wide. The Goddess, Isis, sister-wife of Osiris, and principle of love and magic, searched the lands of the Nile for the dismembered parts, collecting them and bringing together that which had been lost. This story is part of a mythology that guided the Egyptian civilisation for thousands of years. It tells of deepest loss and of recovery through persistence and love.

We also have suffered deep loss. There is much searching and gathering to do to recollect our memories of another way of being as we reconnect to the life-giving power of the Goddess.

Our search can begin with the women who practice mindbody birth control.[4] In the tradition of ancient women's mysteries, these women control conception through a process of internal regulation, without using drugs, synthetic hormones, or physical devices, and without abstaining at any time during the fertility cycle. This method involves an internal mindbody process that allows us to choose whether or not to conceive, regardless of the time in the menstrual cycle, unprotected sex, or any other factors that normally affect reproduction. The result is true reproductive autonomy, a reclaiming of deep inner wisdom and power. It is a practical experience of what can happen when the ancient mysteries of the Goddess are rediscovered and gathered together by modern women.

You may be wondering why there is a need for a new method of birth control in the 21st Century, when reproductive technology has given us birth control methods that claim to offer control and autonomy. The interesting thing is that many women do not experience modern birth control methods as empowering. On the contrary, they speak of feeling controlled and without choice.[5]

In my research I discovered that the key issues for women about their experience of birth control are

- choice vs no choice,
- empowerment vs powerlessness,
- control vs lack of control,
- taking active responsibility vs not assuming active responsibility.

I have heard again and again from women how deeply dissatisfied they are with the mainstream contraceptive choices currently available. While I had expected this from women practising mindbody birth control and other alternative methods, many women using conventional methods are also not happy with their contraceptive choice (or lack of choice).

After using the Pill for many years, Mandy, a journalist in her mid thirties, was still not wanting to have children, but was dissatisfied with her birth control choices.

> *I didn't want to take the Pill and also it didn't agree with me. It did alter my hormones and my mood. Stressed, miserable etc.*

Believing, however, that the Pill was the only reliable contraceptive method, Mandy continued to use it, struggling with the mood changes and distress.

Jane, on the other hand, decided to stop using the Pill which she also associated with mood swings and depression. She was experiencing a change of identity after leaving her work as a teacher to be at home with her pre-school daughter. In her own words,

> *Either the Pill was not helping or it was one more thing where I felt controlled. I gave up on that idea.*

Sophie, a 48 year old with three teenage children, looked back on her childbearing years with a sense of powerlessness described by many women using the Pill,

> *I think there was also the sense of something that was controlling me. It was dictating the cyclical changes in my body. There was a sense of something being added to my system that wasn't me, that was accelerating and exacerbating things. There was a definite mood change, I could feel it when it started to happen around ovulation there was a sense of I suppose you could call it PMT. There was definitely a change. And I really didn't like it at all. I hated the fact that I had to take the Pill, that it had to be in control of me, that I had to use something to control fertility.*

This dislike was echoed by many of the women I spoke with.

Andrea, a nurse who, at 35, had decided to stop at two children, was pleased to be back at work now they were at school. She was, however, not pleased with the birth control she was using.

> *I . . . thought about my relationship with the Pill and . . . was really starting to dread it. The changes in my body, it did something to me emotionally and a thinking or feeling process which was horrible. I really hated it.*

There are also many women who remember times when they had even less choice than is currently available. Christine was a young woman in the seventies when she approached her family doctor for contraceptive advice. She described how

> *the medical profession did not offer options other than the Pill, diaphragm and IUD and they said the Pill was by far the most reliable. But I didn't like the feelings that happened."*

This resigned acceptance of the unacceptable was expressed again and again by women of all ages about the whole range of conventional birth control methods. Many women have told me how unhappy they are with their contraceptive choices. There were, of course, exceptions to this, and I did meet some women who had happily used the Pill for up to fifteen years without a break. Most women did, however, wish that it had been easier, more comfortable, safer and more aesthetic to manage their fertility.

Most of the women who were unhappy with the Pill did not have specific knowledge of the serious personal and environmental consequences of "oestrogen dominance"[6], a problem that has arisen in part from the widespread use of oestrogen-based oral contraceptives. Nevertheless, many women did have an instinctive objection to the Pill.

There are also women who have made the decision to stop using conventional birth control methods but have not found a reliable alternative.

Carol, a naturopath, became disillusioned with the Pill after her own experience and hearing her women patients complain about it, she eventually decided to stop taking the Pill "*on the grounds that it was poisoning my body.*"

Susan, another health care practitioner, also based her decision to come off the Pill on a renewed respect for her body. She was interested to see what difference it would make off the Pill and almost immediately noticed a positive change in body shape.

Repeatedly women said, "*I was determined never to take the Pill or have an IUD again.*" For many this did, however, come after many years of using a contraceptive method with which they were not happy.

These women speak for many of us who have experienced dissatisfaction, powerlessness and lack of choice in birth control. This represents a disenchantment with a technological age that gives with one hand and takes with another.

Enchantment involves a sense of mystery in which we find value, love, and connection with the world. Disenchantment involves a disconnection from these things in a way that leaves us spiritually and emotionally impoverished. For all the gifts of technological development, we now live in a time when there is a disturbing disregard for the rhythms and cycles of Nature, in the world around us and in our bodies.

The mindbody approach to birth control returns choice and control in a simple, accessible form, and is a safe, inexpensive, empowering alternative for women across the world. The only problem is that it is an idea so foreign to us these days that most modern women cannot even imagine doing it. And that is why it is profoundly important to explore it more deeply. . .

Why is something like mindbody birth control so foreign to us? Why is it so frightening? Did women once know about this? What happened to change things? What has been forgotten and lost?

This is not just another book about an idea. I successfully practised mindbody birth control for 30 years, managing my own fertility through an internal process. During this time, I did not use drugs such as the Pill or any contraceptive devices, and I did not need to use any of the alternative methods that involve paying particular attention to the menstrual or moon cycles. With mindbody birth control there is no abstinence during any particular stage of the menstrual cycle. In other words, whether of not I conceived was totally determined by an internal relationship I had developed with the experience of reproduction. The idea to write this book arose from my personal experience with this approach to birth control, from the actual experience of doing something that could not be easily explained by mainstream medical science.

At the age of twenty-six, I had four children aged between 6 months and 8 years, and was not sure how to effectively stop this abundant fertility. I enjoyed pregnancy and mothering, but enough was enough! I also had a tertiary degree with studies in biology, so I was not ignorant about the reproductive cycle or available methods of birth control. I had, however, made a considered decision not to use the contraceptive Pill, and the other conventional methods had proved unreliable or dangerous. Finally, I experienced a major medical emergency as the end result of using an IUD that perforated my uterine wall and had to be surgically removed. Where all available contraceptive methods had failed or were unacceptable, I had to find an alternative way.

Once I had stepped aside from the birth control methods offered by medical science, I entered a different world. In this world I joined the women who have been searching for answers about birth control since the beginning of time. I began to wonder what women had been doing for all the centuries before Western medical science offered the alternatives that I had recently rejected.

• Is it really true that the contraceptive Pill was the first time women had reliable protection from the cycles of gestation and birth?

• Had women once been able to decide for themselves when, where, with whom, and how many children to produce?

• Were there methods of birth control that allowed a woman to have true reproductive autonomy?

My search for the answers has led me on an exciting journey.

In looking for a safe, reliable, empowering birth control method, I first encountered the rhythm method. Thirty years ago in the small Australian city where I lived, this approach came wrapped in a Christian package surrounded with morality and fear of the father God. It did strike me at this stage of seeking alternatives that a father God was probably not the best reference point for female reproductive autonomy. As my wisdom in this area developed over time, I realised what an understatement that was!

There are, of course, now many fertility awareness methods which, when practised with commitment, offer a reliable, safe alternative to conventional birth control methods. These methods also teach women to engage the rhythms and cycles of their bodies and to reclaim reproductive control. An Internet search for "natural birth control" shows just how far this approach has come in twenty-five years. However, at the time when I was searching for the answers to my questions about birth control, I did not have access to this information, and I found myself on a different journey.

I began to read about birth control practices throughout time and across cultures. The more I read, the more I realised that I had been seeing the world through the blinkers of my conditioning, and that my search was about much more than birth control. There are centuries of social, political, cultural, philosophical, and religious influences that affect a woman's experience of birth control, reproduction, and all other aspects of her life. Things are definitely not what they seem.

When we begin to ask questions, we begin to see through the assumptions and laws that have determined our life choices. Taking a close look at these influences is beginning of being able to choose rather than be controlled by factors that are usually invisible and taken for granted. I am focusing here on the practice of a mindbody method of birth control because it is so unusual that it challenges the way we currently think about what's real and what's possible. There is no doubt that cultural beliefs shape our lives[7], and it requires great effort to see beyond what we have been taught to believe.

Despite centuries of conditioning, many of us can sense that things are not what they seem, that the so-called experts don't always know best. One of the things that supports this sort of intuitive knowing is the relationship women have with our bodies via sexuality, menstruation, pregnancy, childbirth, and hands on parenting. Many of the people who write about the feminine journey of inner work say that a relationship with the body is a vital ingredient, that the work must be embodied. So too it was for me; the discovery of a new sort of birth control method arose from considering my body and considering the physical experience of reproduction. What exactly happens when conception occurs? What needs to happen for it not to occur?

These sorts of questions led me into a process of deep contemplation and meditation on the sensations and emotions of conception; exactly where does it happen? what happens? what would stop it happening? Through this process of sensing, questioning, and observing the process in a very intimate, subjective way, I found a way to prevent implantation of the fertilised egg through a totally internal mindbody process. The result is that I did not become pregnant for thirty years after having three children in my twenties, although I was in a sexually active marriage and did not abstain at any particular time of the menstrual cycle, did not use any other form of contraception, and had no reason to believe that either myself or my partner were biologically infertile over this time.

At first I was so delighted to have discovered this approach to birth control that I simply practised it quietly and engaged the demanding task of parenting four young children, re-engaging my career in psychotherapy as time allowed. Then I began to read books on Jungian psychology, and I realised the significance of reclaiming the deep wisdom of the ancient feminine mysteries. By rejecting modern birth control methods and going back to my inner wisdom, I had found my way back to the Great Mother, the archetypal feminine, the Goddess in her many forms.

The feminine mysteries of ages past have been reappearing in the form of archaic figures emerging from archaeological excavations, in the form of images and stories of the goddesses of Old Europe and ancient Greece, and in the form of books and papers on the archetype of the feminine. Over time, as I read many of the books, worked with my dreams, and continued to practice mindbody birth control, I found many links between mindbody birth control and ancient practices from the time of the Goddess.

As I emerged from the period of intensively parenting pre-school children, my focus broadened, and I became interested in mindbody birth control as it related to contemporary culture and to ancient cultures. I began to actively seek other women who might have had similar experiences and to explore the literature for references to reproductive autonomy. It became important to find a context of meaning other than (as well as) the personal for my experience.

My excitement in these new discoveries grew as I met other women who had found their own ways to manage fertility outside the contemporary reproductive beliefs and practices, and I began to wonder how this could become available for women more generally. This book is my answer to all the questions I found myself asking about reclaiming true reproductive autonomy, practising birth control according to the Goddess, and embracing power, choice and control in my life.

The actual practice of mindbody birth control is very simple. The women you will hear from in this book describe ways to prevent conception through an internal process with no outside drugs or interventions. As well as getting to know the Goddess as she appears in my own psyche, I have used imagery and body sensing to prevent implantation of the fertilised egg; another woman says "No" to the spirit of the child wanting to enter; yet another visualises a trapdoor that protects her womb; others describe variations on these processes.

What we all have in common is that
• we are dissatisfied with conventional birth control methods;
• we value choice, control and empowerment in fertility management;

- we are ruthless in our determination to have no (more) children;
- we have actively sought a viable alternative method of birth control;
- we assume this is possible outside the existing forms;
- we approach the alternative practice of birth control with concentration and commitment.
- we experience a permeability between conscious and unconscious processes and experience.
-

What we don't know

If we believe that there was no reliable contraception before the Pill, then it becomes a boon offered to women by medical science, creating a necessary dependence on scientific method and technology.

Is there a problem with this?

Yes. Science and technology have worked to tame, harness, and manage Nature, and there is a relationship between the way in which a culture treats Nature and treats females.

Eco-feminism is very clear that there is a strong link between the denigration of nature and the denigration of the female in Western cultures.[8] I believe that there is also a link between the cultural disregard of women's mysteries over the last 3000 years and women's experience of feeling controlled and disempowered through their use of conventional methods of birth control. As wondrous as they can be, the discoveries of rational science are no substitute for the age-old wisdom of women's mysteries.

There are many references in the literature that suggest that birth control has, in fact, been available throughout human history, and that knowledge of this has been eradicated by social, religious, and cultural factors. In his book on post-conceptive fertility control, one Australian doctor stated that

> medicine has gone to some pains to convert it (fertility control) to an institutionalised matter of tortuous complexity and recoils as much from the idea of simple, painless fertility control on request, as it did from the "heresy" of anaesthesia for childbirth during the last century. [9]

While he is not talking about mindbody control of fertility, this doctor is making the point that things may not be what they seem in the world of conventional birth control. What if simple, self-regulated birth control were actually available to women? How would this affect our lives?

To answer these questions, we need to consider how women have experienced birth control in recent times. Our dependence on medical science is poetically described by Jungian analyst, Irene Claremont de Castillejo[10],

> since the advent of Freud, man's whole attitude towards sexuality has begun to change. It seems that he has more or less digested the apple from the tree of knowledge of good and evil given him by Eve, and, stretching out his hand to the same tree, has plucked a

second apple and this time it is he who has offered it to her. He has discovered the contraceptive . . ..It was Eve who freed Adam from the blindness of nature. Now Adam had freed Eve from the inexorability of its rhythmical wheel.

I disagree. Contemporary contraceptive practices have not, in fact, freed Eve from Nature, but have, very subtly, but very surely, bound her to the relentlessness of science and linearity. Nature is not blind, but can offer a very different way of seeing.

There are numerous examples from the study of linguistics that tell of people living in remote areas who have no words in their languages that are the equivalent of words familiar to people from other cultures. The interesting observation is that without the words, the colours or shapes represented by the words do not exist for these people; when people with no word for "corner" are exposed to what a native English speaker would perceive as a right angle, they see a rounded curve. When we have no word for something, it cannot be seen. It is like that with the idea of effective, self-regulated birth control before the contraceptive Pill.

There have been many ways in which women across cultures have managed fertility, some more effective than others. You will find some of the more efficient methods used in pre-industrial cultures in Part II. It is, however, difficult for modern women, living in a civilised, industrial, technologically advanced culture to accept these methods. Mindbody birth control, with its implication of female reproductive autonomy and female power, seems not to exist in the English language, and is, therefore, omitted from the literature and from the realms of possibility. Yet once the concept exists, there can also be found evidence of its existence. As neuroscientist, Candace Pert, reminds us, "absence of proof is not proof of absence".[11]

Many women recognise mindbody birth control once it is named. They talk about times when it was disastrous or inconvenient to be pregnant, and miraculously the pregnancy did not occur or spontaneously aborted. This is, therefore, something that women are just doing anyway. They just have not known in a fully conscious way what it is they are doing!

Jenny, a mother of three in her late thirties, told me about the time before she was married:

> *I met my husband at 23 and had been sexually active since 18. In that time I did not have any consciousness about this but through this time I was quite sexually active with a number of sexual partners and never in that time practised any form of contraception apart form a vague awareness of the rhythm method. But only vaguely. I was foolish; the only awareness was that I did not want children, but there was no practice or awareness. I did not conceive.*

So many women remember this sort of experience at a time in their lives, often in their late teens or early twenties, when they were sexually active and not ready to settle down and have children. Although there are, of course, the unplanned, unwanted pregnancies, there are also many examples of "lucky escapes". At least some of these events are, in fact, often much more than lucky escapes. They are actually examples of mindbody birth control.

Women are often just doing something intuitively, instinctively, without even realising the power of our experience or the implications for the rest of our lives. Like Jenny, many women describe something that prevented pregnancy when they really did not want to conceive.

Bronwyn, married now with two school-age children, talks about

> *the sexually active times before I was married when there would or would not be forms of contraception. There was a sense that I said "NO" to being pregnant. I don't know what was operating but I never fell pregnant even though there were circumstances like having sex during ovulation . . .and yet I fell pregnant easily once I married.*

This description of something happening to prevent conception appeared again and again in talking with women. As one woman said,

> *When we are really doing things we are just doing them, and then people ask us and we say, "Well, I just do it."*

Mindbody birth control is something that many women are just doing anyway.

As part of my doctoral research, I explored this experience of "something" happening in this way to prevent conception. I collected statements like those from Jenny and Bronwyn, and I then asked other women to rank the statements according to whether they had experienced something similar. Fifty percent of the women I interviewed agreed that there was "something within" operating to prevent pregnancy but usually outside of conscious awareness. These stories of something happening are important because they allow you to recognise that mindbody birth control is not a strange practice accessible to only a few women. It is something that women do anyway. The next step is consciously claiming the right and the capacity to regulate fertility in this way with full conscious awareness, and also realizing the implications for women's experience of power, control and choice.

As well as the women who are just doing it unconsciously, there are women practising mindbody birth control consciously and knowingly. The women who talked with me about their experience were nearly all mothers who had developed their practice as a result of dissatisfaction with conventional birth control methods and a strong desire to have no more children. There was also one younger woman who had been practising mindbody birth control after learning of the method from an older friend. She has since chosen to conceive and was easily able to do so. These women described their experience in different ways:

Jenny, a birth educator in her late thirties with three children, described the deep spiritual basis from which she and her husband *choose not to incarnate any more souls and this is . . .a thought perception rather than physical.*

Sandra, after four children, decided to work consciously through prayer to manage her fertility,

> *At that point there was searching time for me and checking what we wanted. In my asking I asked that if this being was right I would have it, but if it was not necessary I prayed I would not have it. This was with God and also the child. In the end I missed one month and probably about 6 weeks from conception my period came and the baby decided to go. Asking consciously whether this was what we or the baby needed. So the baby passed.*

Following an abortion at nineteen, Chris began searching for a natural birth control method that gave her full control of whether or not she conceived. For her, the experience of mindbody birth control

> i*s situated in my lower belly and there is a trapdoor as the door of contraception. It is a really simple procedure that requires maintenance and constant attending at the end and beginning of each menstrual cycle. Quiet, ancient knowings, very different to the logos time of the 20th century. Yet it transcends time, being very relevant to me in this time. This place of knowledge and peace.*

The practice of mindbody birth control is something that some women around the world have spontaneously developed, sometimes teaching it to others, and sometimes just doing it.

My own experience has been that women are interested in the possibility, but they are very uncertain about trying it for themselves. True autonomy can be frightening, as well as exciting and empowering.

In order to use this simple method of birth control, we have to come to terms with our cultural and personal beliefs about women and power, and we must confront our lack of confidence in the relationship with our deep feminine wisdom. This is not new. Claiming reproductive independence has been fraught with difficulty for European women since recorded history.

A mindbody method of birth control which, by its nature, offers true reproductive autonomy, does not fit our current social, religious, and political beliefs. Even women who consciously challenge these beliefs in some areas of their lives find the idea of taking charge of birth control in this very independent way daunting. What if it doesn't work?

We become bluffed by the shame and fear associated with unwanted pregnancy rather than claiming our right to decide for ourselves.

One of the main factors in practising mindbody birth control is working through the fears and doubts that are an inevitable result of thousands of years of conditioning. Obviously these don't just dissolve like the wicked witch in *Wizard of Oz* when we throw a bucket of water on them (although it is worth a try, as ritual process can be an effective antidote to cultural conditioning). Naming and examining the belief systems and "facts" that we take for granted is a beginning. The sacred tasks in Part II engage this more fully.

However, the first step in approaching mindbody birth control is to seriously consider the idea that women *can* actually regulate their fertility through an internal mindbody process.

The word 'mindbody" is not in the dictionary because we are used to splitting mind and body, and, at best, they are joined with a hyphen (as in mind-body). The process of mindbody birth control is about mind and body working together. It is not about mind over matter, or even mind affecting matter; it involves a recognition that mind and matter are not really separate. Our culture has dismembered these parts, and they must be reconnected.

We are used to thinking of mind and body as separate and to locating our centre of identity in the mind. A long time ago philosophers decided that it was thinking that made us who we are. The famous statement, "I think, therefore I am"[12], was made in the 17th century by a deeply religious young man who was attempting to describe an inner world of mind and soul. Although he was clearly making a distinction between this and the external material world, even Descartes would probably be horrified by the total separation of psyche and matter that has developed from his statement.

Another visionary, analytical psychologist, CG Jung[13], has worked to reconnect psyche and matter, describing them as two aspects of a single, inter-connected reality. Consistent with this, current bio-medical research has revisioned the mindbody relationship as interconnecting systems operating with their own intelligences[14] (more about this in Part IV). These ideas challenge beliefs and attitudes that divide and scatter matter and psyche, body and mind. While there is now a general acceptance that the mind influences the body, and recognition of psychosomatic symptoms is commonplace, this still reflects a fundamental attitude of separation of mind and body. Our language is just beginning to include words that express something of the continuum along which this process occurs: mind-body systems, psycho-neuro-immunological processes. There is a clumsy joining together of parts that have, in all probability, never been separate except in our understanding. It is as if Seth, that ancient Egyptian force of limitation and destruction, has been at work severing mind and body, and we need the Goddess to bring the parts together again.

One of the gifts of the Goddess is the magic of creativity. In engaging this, you will also deepen your relationship with your creativity.

Women practising mindbody birth control are dissatisfied with conventional practices, have a strong motivation to find an alternative, and *believe that this is possible*. This combination of elements is also fundamental to the experience and expression of creativity. In order to be creative, we must first step aside from how things are usually done, how they are usually perceived. We must believe in the possibility of something new emerging onto the canvas or the page, or out of the guitar or the oven.

Creativity has been described as "effective surprise", 'the unexpected that strikes one with wonder or astonishment". [15]

This wonder and astonishment is described by Jeannie, who, in her twenties, experienced a spontaneous abortion after a confirmed, unwanted pregnancy. Effective surprise indeed:

> *Once I made the commitment (to abort the pregnancy) that was definitely what I was going to do and it was a very short amount of time, maybe a day or so after that I was up snorkelling and I just . . .that was it . . .I just let go and I came up out of the water and I was . . .and I had the bleeding . . .I was dancing on top of a rock, I was speechless.*

This sort of experience stirs many questions.

•   When women are regulating conception through an internal mindbody process, what are they doing, how are they doing it, and how did they know what to do?

•   If this is really possible, then how is it that most women do not do this?

•   Have they forgotten?

•   Did they ever know?

•   What was it they may have known?

•   How did they forget?

•   What are the implications of remembering?

I have sought the answers in history, mythology, anthropology, psychology, and biology, and in my own dreams and the "soul stories" of the women who have shared their experiences with me.

The following chapters offer new perspectives and possibilities. The information may stir unconscious responses that shape your experience of the material via dreams, images, memories, and emotional responses that arise while you are reading the book. If you are serious about reclaiming the ancient mysteries and/or exploring mindbody birth control, take the time to read this book slowly, paying attention to your internal responses as well as to the words on the page.

One way to do this is to pause every page or so and breathe deeply, noticing the breath as it moves in and out of your body and also noticing any areas of tightness or holding or of tingling or excitement, or whatever responses are present in your body awareness as you are reading. I also suggest that you keep a journal from when you begin reading, recording dreams, as well as other life events and experiences along the way. Sometimes it is only after a period of time that a theme or story emerges from our subjective experience. Isis spent many moons wandering the ancient land of Egypt, finding the lost parts of Osiris one by one, patiently and lovingly gathering them together, restoring that which had been lost to her. Your task is to gather the bits one by one to form the body of wisdom that connects you to the Goddess and the ancient feminine mysteries.

I am convinced, after 30 years of journeying with this process, that mindbody birth control works. I am also convinced that it needs to come present from the inside out and is likely to encounter some personal and collective resistance on the way. So I invite you to absorb the ideas in this book from the outside in, as well as attending to your own subjective responses as they develop from the inside out.

It is your journey. Take the time to explore the ideas and the practices and find your way to reconnect with the age-old wisdom of the Goddess. You will rediscover a way of being that brings mystery and magic back into the everyday and grounds you in your own deep feminine power.

PART II

HERSTORY THROUGH MYTHOLOGY AND ANTHROPOLOGY

WHAT REALLY HAPPENED TO THE GRANDMOTHERS

CHAPTER TWO

MYTHOLOGY AND HERSTORY
FACT AND FICTION

We learn about history and mythology through the stories that have come to us from the past. Sifting through the various events and tales is like sorting through the clues in a mystery novel. Are things exactly as they seem? Or is there a missing piece of information that changes the way we see things?

My formal education gave me no true understanding of the underlying social, religious, and political forces that make up the current consensus view of reality. As a child, I often saw things differently from the adults. Like so many of us, I learned to put my own perceptions aside and accept the version of reality presented by family and school and television. But I was uneasy; so much did not make sense to me.

Every month my mother drove me to the city to visit the Public Library. I browsed the bookshelves for four books to take home for the month. I can still smell the particular perfume of old paper and wooden bookshelves. As I searched for my books in the half light of the old library, I found a shelf marked *Myths and Legends.* The books were arranged in geographical groups, *Myths and Legends of Ancient Greece, Myths and Legends of Scandinavia,* and so on. In these books I found the stories that made sense of my world, especially my inner world of feelings and fears, of monsters under the bed and evil spirits possessing the people I loved. The myths and legends also confirmed my suspicion that Nature was filled with a living presence that could communicate meaning, and that there were forces at work beyond my rational understanding.

As a natural extension of this early love affair with myths and legends, I rediscovered mythology as I was browsing the bookshelves in the University Library for historical information about birth control. The smell of old paper and wood was familiar, and the stories I found once again made sense of my world. The following section explores our relationship with story, especially the ones we have inherited from our families and culture.

Are you ready to reconsider what you know of the world and your place in it?

The stories from our past have profound implications for us today; they explain how our current beliefs and attitudes have formed over time. There are many clues that have been overlooked in our education. The story of the loss of women's mysteries is the first step in reclaiming our true heritage as daughters of the Goddess. This is not just another passing fad. This is the story of your past, of the events and attitudes that have led us to the brink of losing our connection to the life-giving power of the Goddess. It is also the basic information that can support you in reconsidering your approach to birth control and the whole experience of being a woman in today's world.

Before we look to the past, it is important to understand that mythology is not just about stories from ancient Greece or tales of Celtic heroes. Our current time is also made up of particular myths. However, we call the current myths "reality" or 'truth". Mythology is a collection of stories that includes both fantasy and fact and that provides meaning collectively and personally.[16] When we can recognise that any view of reality is actually the product of a mythology, or a collection of mythologies, we can begin to move beyond some of the unconscious assumptions that determine our lives.

Our strongest myths today come from science and technology. Medical science, for example, teaches us about biological reproduction and the use of the contraceptive Pill. As you will see, this is only one story about fertility and reproduction, and it is a story that denies women true reproductive autonomy.

Do you know why that is the case?

Modern methods of birth control do not offer reproductive autonomy but rather a kind of reproductive dependence that a study of mythology and history places in a disturbing and provocative perspective.

Science is one story we use to make sense of our experience and give it meaning. Science is, however, the dominant myth of our times and, as people in all times have done, we tend to believe in the absolute truth of our own myths. The myths of other times and places explain fertility quite differently from biological science and, as you will see, also offer women different ways to manage their reproductive choices.

A study of mythology, ancient and contemporary, invites us to look at human experience in a broader historical and cultural context than usual. While this sounds like a good idea, it is actually quite difficult to look beyond our own understandings to other ways of experiencing the world. We tend to believe our own stories and be suspicious of others. This is, after all, how cultures have survived for millennia. We are, however, at a time of the world when it could be catastrophic not to listen to other stories. Unless we can learn to interact and exchange as a world-wide community, the destructive potential in human beings will remain a constant threat. This has, of course, been the case through most of recorded history, but now we have the means to perpetrate disaster on a world-wide scale.

History and myth seem to be inextricably intertwined in our thinking. I can remember one of my daughters coming home from primary school with a story of how she had questioned her history teacher about locating an historical event "at the time of Christ". She wanted to know if he was saying that

Christ was an historical figure. The question was shocking to some of her fellow students, simply incomprehensible to others, and even the teacher had trouble answering. This question is, however, one of many that can begin to unravel history as we know it, opening up possibilities by sorting fact from fantasy, without losing the value of either. The Christ energy, for example, is profoundly meaningful to those it touches whether or not there was a proven historical figure called Jesus (the significance lies in the symbolic power to stir meaning and reverence, not necessarily in historical reality). It is, however, vitally important to sort through the underlying assumptions of our belief systems.

Questions like the one my daughter asked may seem irrelevant today when formal religion is not as important to the community as a whole as it once was. Yet just because we have stopped going to church or even consciously believing in a father God, it does not take away the deep influence of a major religion on a culture over time. In a predominantly Christian culture, many of the teaching stories of the Bible still affect us in some way, even if we have not learned them directly.

All people throughout time have had myths of the creation of the world, stories that explained the mystery of life and existence, and each community believed that their story was the true story. Every religious story is a myth that explains the mysteries of life and death according to the people who dreamed it into existence. Even if it we believe that these people received the teachings from a higher power of some sort, they are still formed into stories that reflect the cultural conditions and historical era in which they come present. One of the first steps in claiming autonomy is exploring how the stories of our culture affect us now.

Adam and Eve and Kiss Me went down to the river to bathe; Adam and Eve were drowned, and who do you think was saved?

Children's rhyme

Even those of us who are not actively practising the religion have been influenced by the basic assumptions of the Judeo-Christian myth. Almost everyone knows that the first man was Adam. Most people also think that the first woman was Eve, the one foolish enough (or evil enough) to take the apple from the serpent. What does this story teach as it is absorbed directly or indirectly?

Take a moment to consider the story of Adam and Eve. You may know it in some detail or only vaguely, but it is almost certain that you do know it. What effect does this story have? What does it teach about men and women? If you write what you know of the story from your childhood, how would it go?

Actually stop reading and take some time to write the story as an exercise:

Once upon a time there was a man and a woman called Adam and Eve . . .

Continue the story as you remember it.

Now, reread what you have just written, bearing in mind that this story has been told for centuries as a teaching story about good and evil, men and women. What does your version of the story suggest about life?

The generally accepted version of the story would have us believe that woman, through Eve, brought suffering and sin into our lives by eating the forbidden fruit. But, what exactly was it that Eve ate and tempted Adam to taste as well? Could it have been not only knowledge of good and evil but also wisdom and choice? What do you think?

This, and other stories like it, have the power to shape our lives. Can you think of other cultural myths that contain underlying messages that form your view of the world? Make a list of these and examine what they tell you.

One of the most insidious cultural myths that affect women today is the well-known "beauty myth"[17]. The constant bombardment of slim, athletic, youthful images of women has a profound effect on our ability to be comfortable in our own bodies. When we are not able to be comfortably and fully embodied, we have no real internal ground on which to stand to make informed, empowering choices. Do you believe the story told by the beauty myth? Or do you spend life energy holding it at bay?

The beauty myth has the power to affect your ability to trust yourself and claim your deep feminine wisdom. Our instinctual knowings are often not particularly fashionable or attractive according to contemporary ideas of beauty. Women today are caught in a paradox: even while we are struggling to develop our full potential in the work place, in relationship and family, or in areas of creativity, at the same time many of us are concerned about being too big. The contradiction is terrible: I want to be as big as I can be, but I also want to be smaller. This struggle undermines us as effectively as the old injunctions of the Dark Ages, limiting our capacity to develop a full experience of feminine power and autonomy.

The origins of the beauty myth predate the feminist movement by thousands of years; they are inextricably linked to changing mythological conditioning regarding the value of the life-giving power of the feminine. When fertility is highly valued in a culture, women have reproductive power, but once the value of fertility is displaced by economic, political, or military values, there is a shift in sexual emphasis from fertility to erotic power. When the life-giving power of the feminine is devalued, the value of women's bodies changes. In the words of cultural historian, William Irwin Thompson, "Gone is the obese Great Goddess; come is the sleek young maid…" [18]

How we think and act is profoundly influenced by the stories and images of our culture. Much of the current education and practice of birth control reflects contemporary myths rather than our authentic subjective experience of our bodies, desires, and deepest understandings. As we have seen, many women report a dissatisfaction with conventional methods of birth control, even while believing they have no choice with this.

In her book on *The Scapegoat Complex*, Silvia Brinton Perera recounts a story from the Sufi tradition, the esoteric school of Islam. I retell *The Wayward Princess* here as it is a metaphor for seeing through the existing laws to find a new way of experiencing the world.

A certain king believed that what he had been taught, and what he believed, was right. In many ways he was a just man, but he was one whose ideas were limited. One day he said to his three daughters: "All that I have is yours or will be yours. Through me you obtained your life. It is my will which determines your future, and hence determines your fate."

Dutifully, and quite persuaded of the truth of this, two of the girls agreed. The third daughter, however, said: "Although my position demands that I be obedient to the laws, I cannot believe that my fate must always be determined by your opinions."

"We shall see about that," said the king. He ordered her to be imprisoned in a small cell, where she languished for years. Meanwhile the king and his obedient daughters spent freely of the wealth which would otherwise have been expended on her. The king said to himself: 'this girl lies in prison not by her own will, but by mine. This proves, sufficiently for any logical mind, that it is *my* will, not hers which is determining her fate."

The people of the country, hearing of their princess's situation, said to one another: "She must have done or said something very wrong for a monarch, with whom we find no fault, to treat his own flesh and blood so." For they had not arrived at the point where they felt the need to dispute the king's assumption of rightness in everything.

From time to time the king visited the girl. Although she was pale and weakened from her imprisonment, she refused to change her attitude.

Finally, the king's patience came to an end. "Your continued defiance," he said to her, "will only annoy me further, and seem to weaken my rights, if you stay within my realms. I could kill you; but I am merciful. I therefore banish you into the wilderness adjoining my territory. This is a wilderness, inhabited only by wild beasts and such eccentric outcasts who cannot survive in our rational society. There you will soon discover whether you can have an existence apart from that of your family and, if you can, whether you prefer it to ours."

His decree was at once obeyed, and she was conveyed to the borders of the kingdom. The princess found herself set loose in a wild land which bore little resemblance to the sheltered surroundings of her upbringing. But soon she learned that a cave would serve for a house, that nuts and fruit came from trees as well as golden plates, that warmth came from the Sun. This wilderness had a climate and a way of existing of its own.

After some time she had so ordered her life that she had water from springs, vegetables from the earth, fire from a smouldering tree. "Here," she said to herself, "is a life whose elements belong together, form a completeness, yet neither individually nor collectively do they obey the commands of my father the king."

One day a lost traveller - as it happened a man of great riches and ingenuity - came upon the exiled princess. They fell in love and journeyed back to his country, where they were married. After a space of time, the two decided to return to the wilderness where they built a huge and prosperous city where their wisdom, resources and faith were expressed to their fullest possible extent. The "eccentrics" and other outcasts, many of them thought to be madmen, harmonised completely and usefully with this many-sided life.

The city and its surrounding countryside became renowned throughout the entire world. It was not long before its power and beauty far outshone that of the realm of the princess's father. By the unanimous choice of the inhabitants, the princess and her husband were elected to the joint monarchy of this new and ideal kingdom.

At length the king decided to visit the strange and mysterious place which had sprung up in a wilderness, and which was, he heard, peopled at least in part by those whom he and his like despised. As, with bowed head, he slowly approached the foot of the throne upon which the young couple sat and raised his eyes to meet those whose repute of justice,

> **prosperity and understanding far exceeded his own, he was able to catch the murmured words of his daughter.**
>
> **"You see, Father, every man and woman has his own fate and his own choice."** [19]

The Wayward Princess shows us that we can find new laws by which to live, laws that are not determined by the dominant beliefs and values of the "father" world. This mythic tale links us to the autonomy of the most ancient Goddesses whose laws predate those of a father God.

The Goddess as she appears in mythology can remind us of different ways to make sense of our experience. It has been a delight to introduce the stories of the ancient Goddesses to women in my clinical psychotherapy practice over the years. What a relief it has been for them to discover so many aspects of the feminine that give permission for new ways of experiencing themselves and the world.

Myths can also describe the sometimes dramatic breakthrough of the sacred, or supernatural, into the world, bringing present mythical figures and stories that describe the functions of the feminine principle in creation and procreation. Among the mythic figures that women encounter is Lilith, the first woman in the Judeo-Christian story of creation. She comes as a surprise to most women as they have never heard of her. She was well and truly banished from the Garden of Eden for her "disobedience", even before Eve appeared. As I describe more fully in Part III, Lilith entered my life through a dream and has guided my journey of rediscovering the ancient wisdom of the feminine.

The following image is a life size drawing that hangs on the wall in my therapy room. Lilith has become a guide for many of the women who meet her there or in their own dreams.

Lilith. Original in acrylic, pencil, ink. Author.

At first she can be disturbing with her mouth wide open, screaming, her hair flying wildly about her head, eyes blazing, nails long and red. Yet a remarkable number of women recognise this archetypal image and come to know her as an inner teacher of ancient mysteries. She is the Wayward Princess's many times great, great Grandmother. And yours.

Lilith's story is the story of the first woman, our most ancient mother. Until a few years ago, this story was almost lost to us. Along with the ways of the ancient mothers, Lilith had been cast out of our memories. In the oldest of Old Testaments, Lilith was the first woman, created in her own right. Not from a rib of Adam. She knew the name of God and could choose her own path. When Adam tried to force her to lie under him for sex, she left the Garden of Eden. Next came Eve, more compliant yet still disobedient enough to listen to the serpent.

Some say that it was Lilith who returned in the form of the serpent, offering Eve a choice: To live in the Garden of the Father God in ignorance of her true identity as a daughter of the Goddess, or to remember her birthright and find her way back.

Eve chose to take a bite of the apple, and woman was cursed by the Father God for Eve's disobedience. The curse condemned women to bear their children in pain and to live under their husband's rule (the Father God claiming dominion over women's business).

As daughters of Eve, we are now faced with a choice: Do we continue to live under this ancient curse? Or do we call to Lilith and find out where She has been all this time?

There are many modern women who would say that they are already free of Eve's curse. They are independent and can choose whether or not to bear children at all. And, if they do, there is pain relief on hand.

The only problem is that somewhere in this freedom, something fundamental has been lost. Where are the mother's ways? Where is the ancient pact between women and the Goddess?

As Marion Woodman says, modern women have learned to '"take it like a man" in order to achieve independence and success in the world. This includes modern methods of contraception that are based on principles of science and medical technology.

This may still seem like a fair trade.

Except that

• women in developed countries now consider losing weight a major life goal,

• eating disorders have risen exponentially in the last thirty years,

• cosmetic surgery for women has become the fastest growing medical speciality[20],

• between 10-20% of women experience post-natal depression[21],

- human trafficking has become a global business, with between 700,000 and 2 million women trafficked across international borders annually.[22]

Something is terribly wrong!

I have written this book to speak out against the imbalance of the last two thousand years, to call for women to return to the way of the Mother. This is not a romantic or sentimental book. Some women who have read it find themselves restless, sleeping badly, waking from nightmares. It asks you to assume responsibility at a very fundamental level for the life-giving power bestowed by the Goddess. We have been giving this away for so long that it can be terrifying to reclaim our birthright as daughters of Lilith.

Once she was replaced by the slightly more obedient Eve, Lilith no longer existed in our teaching stories, or our conscious thoughts. Yet there she is at the very beginning. The original Old Testament story tells us that Lilith left the Garden of Eden, never to return, and she has, therefore, been left out of the story as we know it today. She only appears as a hag, inhabiting the outer regions, giving birth to demons and luring men and women into depravity. She is there, waiting for us to dream her and the ancient mysteries back into our lives.

Are you willing to risk depravity?

CHAPTER THREE

ACCORDING TO THE GODDESS

Goddesses rather than male deities were the central focus in European religion from about 6500 BC to 3500 BC. Archaeologist, Marija Gimbutas[23], was one of the first scholars to recognise the significance of the fact that twenty times more female than male figurines have been excavated from European archaeological sites. The many engravings, reliefs and sculptures frequently de-emphasised facial features, while exaggerating gender characteristics such as breasts, buttocks, hips, and vulva. These female figurines had traditionally been seen by archaeologists as some sort of sexual fetishes, a projection of the current degraded view of feminine.

Risking disfavour with the established view, Gimbutas argued that the portrayal of these features of the female human body over a period of more than 20,000 years of our history points to a profoundly important philosophical idea. She understood that the Neolithic images are symbolic or mythical figures, probably used to commemorate seasonal or other rites dedicated to the various aspects of the "Goddess Creatrix"[24], the Goddess in her many forms.

The people of those ancient times were probably more practical than philosophical about the Goddess, clearly recognising and celebrating their profound interdependence with Nature and the feminine principle. Just as women could produce new life from within their bodies, so could Nature renew life each spring and provide abundantly each summer. The sheer number of the figurines shows us that honouring the feminine principle was fundamental to people's lives for about 25,000 years of our pre-history.

The Great Mother.
Original in pastel. Rena Hoffman.

Some of the earliest symbolic representations of the feminine principle are engravings and drawings of vulvas from the Aurignacian period, 35,000 years ago. The artist appears to have been making a symbol, "not of human birth alone but of all birth in nature".[25] The functions of both Nature and woman, especially birth and regeneration, belonged to the mysterious world of the Goddess, the feminine principle.

This deep reverence for the feminine has obviously changed over the last three thousand years. There are now many books written about the takeover of women's mysteries by patriarchal rulership of state and church.[26] While there is little doubt about the meaning of patriarchal (male dominated), there is often confusion about the structure of the historical cultures in which the Goddess was worshipped. It is tempting to swing to the idea of a matriarchy in which the feminine principle, and therefore women, were dominant. This, however, is not strongly supported by researchers in this area.

There is considerable support for the existence of cultures in which there was a respect for the life-giving power of the Goddess with no particular superiority of either sex. Rather than a time when women were dominant, it seems more likely that there was a time when society was unstratified and equalitarian with no marked distinctions based on either class or sex, and when the life-giving powers of Nature were given the highest value by both men and women. It was in this environment, where the life-giving power of the feminine was respected, that I believe true reproductive autonomy was practised.

Even as the feminine principle was venerated for its fertile, life-giving properties, there are also many examples of Goddesses who embodied the entire life process: birth, life, death, and regeneration. This is important because it can be tempting to romanticise the Goddess as a sort of angelic Fairy Godmother or abundant Good Mother. The feminine principle is more complex and more powerful than that. There are many stories from mythology that tell of the different faces of the Goddess.

One such myth tells of the ancient Sumerian goddess who "outweighed, overshadowed, and outlasted them all . . .Inanna, Queen of Heaven."[27]

This story originated in ancient Mesopotamia, five or six thousand years ago. In the myth, Inanna, who rules as queen over the upper world (birth and life), decides to visit Ereshkigal, queen of the Underworld (death and transformation). As Inanna descends into her sister's realm, she is stripped of all the symbols of her upper world sovereignty, so that she comes before Ereshkigal naked and bowed low. Her enforced stay in the Underworld and the return after three days predates the Christian story by thousands of years. It is one of the first stories of ritual descent from the realm of life to the realm of death and the return to life after a time of incubation in the Underworld. This is also the theme of most ancient initiation rituals like the Orphic mysteries, the Eleusinian mysteries, and of much of the Egyptian sacred teachings.

At the time when the story of Inanna's journey first appeared, the increasingly male dominated Sumerian culture was separating from earlier matrilineal forms. Before the descent myth, another story tells how Inanna, in order to rule, had to take power from the God, Enki, assuming his symbols of sovereignty as her own. Ereshkigal, queen of the Underworld, represents the archaic feminine, the dark mysteries of the older religion which had been sent underground. The descent story can, therefore, be understood as Inanna balancing her heroic victories in the upper (masculine) world by reconnecting with the rhythms and cycles of the under (feminine) world. Based on clinical experience, one analyst called this a "pattern of a woman's passage from cultural adaptation to an encounter with her essential nature".[28]

Inanna's story is a fitting metaphor for women's experience with mindbody birth control. To truly engage conscious internal regulation of fertility, we have to turn our ear to the "great below" as did Inanna, and we must consciously embark on a journey away from rational, upper world understanding.

The Goddess in Inner Work

The ancient myth of Inanna's descent has become important to women who are called to explore the archaic face of the feminine and to balance the heroic upper world approach to life with a time of reflection and incubation. There is profound meaning for us today in Inanna's decision to enter the Underworld and be deeply affected by the mysteries of the dark feminine. I have worked with this myth using ritual to re-engage Inanna's journey, and it is an extraordinary experience to reenact the descent and feel the Goddesses coming to life in response.

Over the years I have worked with groups of women to build a temple space which, as much as we can imagine and guess from ancient images and engravings, is similar to an ancient Sumerian temple of Inanna. Within this *temenos* or sacred space, we reenact the story of Inanna's descent with its experience of death and rebirth. The women engaging these ritual processes encounter the Goddess in Her many forms.

One encounter that stays with me happened during my first enactment of the myth. About half way through a 14-day retreat, I was sitting in silent meditation in the temple space when something prompted me to open my eyes. Walking directly towards me was the largest spider I have ever seen. This was not just a big spider, it was huge! It was actually hard to find a jar or bowl large enough to catch it and relocate it to a tree outside. It was very unusual for a spider to be making such determined progress in broad daylight across the open floor in a room full of people. What I later discovered was that it was also making its way directly to the place set up behind a screen for Ereshkigal, Queen of the Underworld. Spiders are a symbol of the Goddess as the spinner and weaver of fate, and I am sure that this one was not an accidental visitor to the temple.

Over the years, I have worked in therapy with many women who have come to respect the visits from the Goddess in her spider form, both in dreams and waking encounters. Even when they are uneasy in Her presence and prefer to relocate Her out of the house, the encounter with the spider is an opportunity to reconnect with the archaic feminine in the midst of the modern world. We lose a valuable connection if we automatically kill these messengers before paying attention to the authentic emotional response they have the power to evoke. Some of the women who have journeyed to Ereshkigal's realm in ritual space describe the experience of encountering the dark Goddess as very much like coming upon a large spider unexpectedly. Nature provides us with opportunities to feel the presence of the Goddess in our lives, and our encounters with spiders are just one way She reminds us of her existence.

Once again during a descent ritual retreat, Nature presented me with another encounter with the Goddess, this time in her Medusa form. One of the ritual processes involved making a representation of the string of lapis lazuli beads Inanna wore around her throat as a symbol of her upper world sovereignty. As I was making my necklace, I experienced severe constriction in my throat. This eventually cleared through some body work that involved an expression of yelling, screaming, and crying. I felt greatly relieved by the release of the fear and rage that had been held in my throat. Next morning, as I walked past the exact spot where this had happened, there was a Medusa-like cluster of spit-fire caterpillars. These long, black writhing wasp larvae group together in a remarkable imitation of Medusa's hair and are named for the acidic fluid they spit in defense. They are usually found hanging from the branch of a tree but, in this case, there was no tree nearby!

It is very easy to dismiss this sort of experience or my encounter with the spider as nothing but a strange coincidence, or as me reading too much into the event. That is our rational, logos function speaking, that which would deny the living relationship with Nature, deny the manifestation of the extraordinary in the ordinary which is one way the Goddess speaks to us. When I have worked for any length of time with a group of women, there are so many of these meaningful coincidences, from the sublime to the ridiculous, that I am certain this is one way we can experience the sacred in the everyday.

One of the lighter examples of this happened in a dream group where eight women met weekly for several months to work with their dreams. In one woman's dream there was a scene with two Portuguese women lounging on a bed. At the time they were just one curious part of a long, interesting dream. The next day, however, someone visiting me said that she had been going to bring some Portuguese tarts for us to eat. Imagine my surprise! I had never heard of these delicious pastries, and she was not a part of the dream group. The following week there was an article on Portuguese tarts in the epicure section of the morning paper. We have still not solved the mystery of the Portuguese women in the dream, but we did enjoy a feast of homemade tarts in the dream group a few weeks later.

Meaningful coincidence

These coincidences happen to remind us of the sacred in the everyday. Take some time to notice these in your own life and catch the rational mind response that would dismiss the experience as "nothing but". When we attend to these meaningful coincidences, we know who is on the telephone before answering it, or we find ourselves thinking of an old friend just before running into her in the street.

Keep a log book of these sort of meaningful coincidences and learn to recognise the extraordinary in the ordinary, the small life events that remind us of the interconnections of matter and psyche. By learning to take these sort of experiences seriously, we are connecting to an expanded

sense of ourselves that links us to Psyche as World Soul (Anima Mundi).

Meeting the Goddess

My relationship with the Goddess has been a central part of practising mindbody birth control. In my own experience of confronting who or what determined whether or not I would conceive, it was like an internal dialogue with someone or something much bigger and more powerful than myself who was somehow responsible for things like conception and pregnancy and birth and death. This Goddess figure seemed to demand procreation from me (and other women), and my relationship with Her had to change in order to be able to choose not to conceive. Sometimes this was frightening or awesome; at other times it was just what was happening.

This sort of engagement and negotiation with the Goddess is what pre-industrial people did in their ritual practices through the shamans and wise ones of the tribe, and what Jung described in his writing on archetypes. For me, a relationship with the Goddess was vital in practising mindbody birth control. I experienced a force that wanted me to conceive, an instinctual natural energy interested in fertility and abundance, in propagation of the species. It was up to me to claim my individual ground in the face of this and to develop relationship with the Great Mother as I experienced Her. I had to find a way to honour Her without letting Her have all of me.

I developed a small daily ritual of going out into the garden each evening when my four children were finally asleep. I made a small grotto under a large old plum tree, and there I would pour water from an old earthenware jug into a clay bowl with a sense of honouring that aspect of the Goddess that is Nature. I would, through words, song and movement tell Her that I respected and loved Her, but that I could not just let Her take me over and keep me making babies. It was an ongoing negotiation on an internal, energetic level. I learned that there is a strength in creating a sacred space for dialoguing with the Goddess from the personal ground of being human. Claiming this personal ground opens the way for engagement with the bigger energies that otherwise influence our lives unconsciously and automatically.

While the Great Mother certainly represented my instinctual drive to reproduce, I am sure that She is also more than that. It is a mistake to reduce the archetypal feminine to nothing but a representation of our biological or instinctual energies. This is an important choice point in working with the Goddess, and I discuss it more fully in Part IV. For me, the Goddess does exist autonomously, other than as a representation of my inner drives and desires. She is much more than my construction or an image conjured up by my unconscious to explain my biology.

The living presence of the Goddess is something women are learning to recognise in their lives. I have introduced many women to the idea of a daily ritual for the purpose of acknowledging and honouring a Goddess energy while also claiming individual personal ground.

Helen was thirty-two when she first came to therapy. A very attractive woman who deeply desired marriage and family, she had nevertheless made a vow to never have another relationship. She had just emerged from an affair with yet another man who had promised commitment but left as soon as the relationship became more personal. Through her dreams, Helen discovered Aphrodite, the Goddess of love and beauty, at work in her relationships. She made an altar to Aphrodite and lit a candle to the Goddess every day. For Helen, the struggle was not with pregnancy but with repeated relationships with married men who were attracted to her beauty but never fulfilled their promises of a deeper commitment. She worked to develop conscious relationship with this aspect of the Goddess so that she was not always the "other woman" but could choose to become a wife and mother. Since engaging this ritual work, she has married and has two much loved children. While Aphrodite is not as central in Helen's life as previously, she is still a beautiful woman who has access to her sexuality and can choose to fully engage relationship, another of Aphrodite's gifts.

For Melanie, a company director at thirty seven, success in the corporate world was leaving her exhausted and somehow dissatisfied with life. For her the acknowledgement was to Athena, the Goddess born fully formed from her father's head. Melanie's daily ritual involved turning a page of one of her technical books that sat open in front of a picture of Athena on a small altar at home, acknowledging this aspect of the Goddess and explaining that she needed time and energy for other activities. This practice freed her from the inevitability of this archetypal force, allowing her time to develop her creative expression through art as well as maintaining her work.

Donna had a different problem. She had completed a degree in marketing but felt limited in her ability to find meaningful work in the world. She had started several jobs over the last few years, only to find that she could not sustain the work. She had been diagnosed with Chronic Fatigue Syndrome but sensed that something was at work to rob her of the energy she needed to achieve her goals. She identified a devouring "dark mother" energy through her dreams and active imagination. Donna experienced this energy as killing off her confidence and initiative, leaving her drained and bloodless. Her ritual consisted of an offering of fresh chopped liver that she placed outside her back door every evening, inviting the dark mother to eat this rather than attack her. It may have been the local birds that ate it each night, but Donna was quite happy with the new freedom of movement and confidence that entered her life. The shamans and wise ones in pre-industrial cultures have long understood that the birds, insects and animals are one face of the God and Goddess in Nature.

Unless we engage the archetypal energies consciously through ritual and negotiation, they can run our lives with moods, acting out, cravings and addictions.

Honouring the Goddess

Performing a daily ritual is one way to enter into relationship with the ancient feminine. The place where it is conducted will depend on the available space and the face of the Goddess you are working with.

Identify the Goddess energy at work in your life.
You may be able to name this yourself from dream images or life experiences, or you can search in these two excellent books for descriptions of the Goddesses of ancient Greece:

J S Bolen, 1984, <u>Goddesses in Everywoman: A new Psychology of Women</u>, San Francisco: Harper & Row.

J B Woolger & R J Woolger, 1990, <u>The Goddess Within: A Guide to the Eternal Myths That Shape Women's Lives</u>, London: Rider.

Of course, the ancient feminine energy in your life may not fit one of these Goddesses, and you may need to search further afield for her origins in the mythology of other lands. Take into account your own ethnic background. For some people, the Goddesses of Nordic mythology or the Hindu pantheon make more sense of their experience than the deities of ancient Greece. The Goddesses from Ancient Sumer or Egypt have less of the patriarchal overlay than the Goddesses of ancient Greece. Let your authentic images and experiences be your guide. The Goddess image that comes to you may not have an official name or mythological identity. Welcome her anyway!

Make or find an image or symbol of the Goddess figure and place it on an altar.

 Your place of offering can be a mantlepiece or a window sill or a more elaborate altar space you make especially for this purpose. No one but you need know what it is you do there each day. Light a candle, pour water from one container to another, add a river pebble each day to pile of stones, or make an offering of food or drink. While doing this, acknowledge this aspect of the ancient feminine and also declare your personal need or desire ("I honour you but you can't have all of me" is the general theme). Like Helen, Melanie, and Donna, you can develop your own living relationship with the Goddess through regular practice. Remember, mindbody birth control and personal autonomy is not about mind over matter but about a living relationship with matter as Mater . . . as Mother . . . as guide to the mysteries.

Mantlepiece or shelf altar

Lilith and ancient mother Goddess figures

Table altar for the element of water

The Wise Blood of the Goddess: The Menstrual Taboo

The archaic, instinctual feminine, represented by Ereshkigal in the Sumerian myth, appears in many forms in mythology across cultures and time. In the form of the Hindu goddess, Devi or Kali, this feminine principle has two faces: destruction and regeneration. In the form of the Medusa she has been known as the Destroyer aspect of the Triple Goddess called Neith in Egypt, Ath-enna or Athene in North Africa[7]. It is through the Medusa that mythology offers a hint of what may once have been possible for women in terms of birth control.

Medusa's inscription at Sais called her 'mother of all the gods, whom she bore before childbirth existed".[29] The hidden, dangerous face of the Medusa is said to have represented Death, which no mortal can see without being turned to stone. Another interpretation is that Medusa was veiled because she was the Future that is hidden from human view. Yet another meaning of her dangerous face was the menstrual taboo.[30] An early work on mythology described how pre-industrial people often believed that the look of a menstrual woman could turn a man to stone.[31] The Medusa was understood to have magic blood that could create and destroy life, and that represented the dreaded life and death giving "moon-blood" of women. A female face surrounded by serpent-hair was an ancient, widely recognised symbol of divine feminine wisdom, and equally of the "wise blood" that gave women their powers.

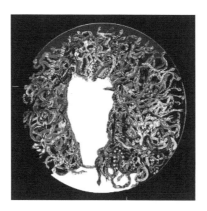

Medusa.
Original in pencil. Lisa McGuire

If the power of Medusa's wise blood is explored, it becomes obvious that menstrual blood represented the mysterious magic of creation from the earliest of human cultures. It is understandable that men may have developed a superstitious dread for women's monthly bleeding, as they saw the life-blood leave the body without any apparent wounding and no pain, an experience unknown to them.[32] Even the words for menstruation in many early cultures meant things like incomprehensible, supernatural, and sacred. At the time when all Gods were seen to recognise the supremacy of the archetypal Great Mother, who manifested as the spirit of creation, her menstrual blood was central to their power. These are potent descriptions of a time (mythological and/or historical) when "God was a woman"[33], when the prevailing myths told of feminine power and mysteries, and when the secrets of fertility resided totally with women.

While the actual process of conception as Western science knows it was often poorly understood, it is recorded that menstrual blood was associated with creation in many cultures, although not in the way we understand it today. The Maoris stated explicitly that human souls are made of menstrual blood which, when retained in the womb, "assumes human form and grows into a man".[34] Some Africans also believed that menstrual blood "congealed to fashion a man".[35] Even in Western medicine, the prenatal function of menstrual blood as either forming the human baby, or at least nourishing it, was also prevalent well into the 19th century. You may be surprised to realise that this was only disproved in 1930.[36]

In other times and places, whether or not a baby was made seemed totally dependent on the functions of the woman's body, and was strongly associated with the cycles of the moon and with feminine deities. One anthropologist observed that

> the idea that menstruation is <u>caused </u>by the new moon is universal. Papuans say that a girl's first menstruation is due to the moon having had connection with her during sleep, and the Maoris speak of menstruation as "moon sickness". A Maori stated: "the moon is the permanent husband, or true husband, of all women, because women menstruate when the moon appears. According to the knowledge of our ancestors and elders, the marriage of a man and wife is a matter of no moment; the moon is the real husband". We shall see that such conceptions are by no means peculiar to the Maori, but pervade primitive thought.[37]

This sort of belief fostered a deep reverence for the life-giving power of the feminine; the relationship between women and Nature was mysterious and sacred.

CHAPTER FOUR

THE POWER OF CREATION

The Maori people respected the importance of the wise blood and the feminine in giving life. It was not a problem for them that the life-giving power rested with women, but this was not always the case.

Male jealousy of women's powers has a long history. An ancient Chinese myth tells the story of the Moon-goddess, Chang-O, who controlled menstruation. Chang-O was so offended by male jealousy of her powers that she left her husband, who quarrelled with her because she had all the elixir of immortality, the menstrual blood, and he had none.[38] Chang-o's solution was to leave earth and take up residence as the moon. In other cultures, women have not been so lucky.

Male jealousy of women's life-giving powers can be seen in the superstitious horror of menstrual blood that pervaded the teachings of Persian and Jewish patriarchs. There have been many taboos forbidding men to touch a menstrual woman, or to wash in water in which she had bathed. From mythology we can see that menstrual blood represented women's access to mysteries and to power unavailable to males. Later Judeo-Christian teachings were apparently influenced by these superstitions and taboos, commanding women to despise the "uncleanness" of their own bodies, and insisting that the power of creating life rested with God and the Church, and not with women. The Church interpreted the teachings of the Bible, particularly the stories in Genesis, as evidence of God's (and, therefore, man's) right to compel women to bear as many children as possible.[39] The unwanted children were often left with the Church to care for or dispose of, a stern reminder that the power of life (and death) rested with a male God, not with women

The transition from matrifocal to patriarchal societies and religions involved a shift of power from feminine principles to masculine, and involved a determined attempt to take the power of creation from the feminine. Cultural historian, William Irwin Thompson, has said that

> this effort to displace the female seems to be the archetypal foundation for civilisation, for mankind has been at it ever since; whether he is challenging mother nature in flying away from her in rockets, or in challenging her on earth through genetic engineering, man has not given up the attempt to take away the mystery of life from the Great Mother and the conservative feminine religion.[40]

Thompson tells the story of another ancient Sumerian myth in which Enki, the god of water, is struggling with Ninhursag, the goddess of earth. This story, like the myth of Inanna, has been translated from inscriptions on stone tablets[41] dating back to around 2500 BC. It tells of the conflict between masculine and feminine in the transition from the Neolithic matrilineal order to the patriarchal.

Enki, a powerful god who can flow over boundaries, inseminating his daughters and the daughters of his daughters, seduces Ninhursag's daughter. Ninhursag takes his semen from her daughter's body and eight plants grow from this. Enki finds the plants, eats them, and finds himself pregnant with eight beings gestating in different parts of his body. He soon becomes ill as he is not made to be pregnant. Ninhursag helps Enki by placing him in her vagina, where he is able to give birth to the eight goddesses. This myth describes Enki's power but also what happens to this when he tries to take over the life-giving power of the feminine. Enki is brought back to the ancient symbol of feminine mysteries, the vulva.

A more recent, and more successful, attempt to displace the feminine occurred with the Inquisition, the Roman Catholic ecclesiastical tribunals for suppression of heresy, which began in the ninth century and lasted for about 600 years. Women, or men, who defied the edicts of the Church, sometimes in apparently trivial ways, were labelled witches or heretics, and murdered. The witchcraft or heresy trials were horrifying in their obvious injustice and brutality, and the number of victims during the "Burning Days"[42] is estimated between 100,000 and 9 million[43]. While the exact numbers are unknown, it seems extraordinary that there is so much uncertainty about exactly what happened in these times. It is not easy to look at our history and see the ignorant, brutal, and destructive forces that have shaped our beliefs and attitudes.

Anyone who had an unusual ability, or who was vocal in criticism of the church or of patriarchal values and laws, risked torture and death. The persecution of so called witches illustrates the determination to destroy or force submission from anyone who threatened patriarchal values. Many churchmen believed that these "witches" inherited secret knowledge of birth control practices, and, as control of conception and fertility posed a threat, this contributed to the vigour of the persecutions.

The *Malleus Malefi Carum*[44], also known as *The Witches" Hammer*, was the definitive text published by the Catholic Church in 1494 to identify witches, define witchcraft, and detail the steps to be taken in eradicating them. I found an old copy of this book in a second hand bookshop and spent many hours incredulously reading the bizarre logic of the misogynist 15th Century priests. They were convinced that

> witches can obstruct the generative powers (copulation) so that intercourse is not possible and babies not conceived,

and that

> sometimes the woman is caused to be unable to conceive by the actions of a witch.

They decreed that

the use of contraceptives such as potions or herbs that contravene nature...are to be punished as homicides.

Overall, they decided,

it is witchcraft, not only when anyone is not able to perform the carnal act . . .but also when a woman is prevented from conceiving".

The message to women was that if you persist in assuming responsibility for birth control and continue to exercise any power or choice in this matter, you will be tortured and/or killed violently.

The terrible reality is that even for those of us who are not currently in such situations of physical danger, the abuses of the Inquisition are not so far away. It is not so many generations ago that women throughout Europe were subject to systematic extermination for practising reproductive autonomy and other independent or creative acts. Not only were the women of those generations (600 years of them) culled for intelligence, creativity, originality, healing ability and autonomy, subsequent generations carried the effects of this persecution, gradually forgetting the cause but nevertheless restricting activities to parameters acceptable to Church and State authorities.

This age-old hostility toward women's life-giving powers still acts as a disincentive to empowerment today, in obvious ways such as religious fundamentalism and radical puritanism, and also less obviously in women's attitudes to body image, the role of mothering, and to fertility management. It is not surprising that women have "forgotten" what is possible in terms of reproductive independence, and experience a lack of confidence in using mindbody birth control. Centuries of conditioning have taught us that it is not safe to trust our instinctual mindbody wisdom, whether in healing, birthing practices, or contraception.

The Roman Catholic doctrine against all forms of birth control is based on the views of a few significant thinkers like Thomas Aquinas (1225-1274), a theologian who claimed that contraception was not only morally wrong but also unnatural, and Augustine, Bishop of Hippo, in the late fourteenth century. It is shocking that their thinking has so profoundly influenced how we see the world today, especially when we remember that their view of women was

> not so much as the creators but simply as the custodians of the progeny they carry within their bodies.[45]

The same scripture that cursed woman for Eve's sin and denied women as life-givers, also forbade access to teachings and mysteries associated with women's business. The original curse has been interpreted and elaborated by generations of fanatical priests who were determined to leave women without choice or power. They have successfully eradicated direct access for women to the mythological potency of the "inexhaustible power of creation".[46]

This power of creation was taken over by the Church as its own, and any ability to control conception represented a threat to patriarchal or church control. The Inquisition concentrated much of its efforts on attempts to totally eradicate the theory and practice of fertility regulation. It is ironical that during the 1960's, medicine rediscovered techniques, and began to adopt attitudes that were well understood and accepted more than 2,500 years ago.[47] It is now recognised by medical researchers that there has been an obvious discontinuity of knowledge regarding birth control, while many rediscoveries have yet to be made.[48]

For many of the people in European pre-history, before the catastrophic losses of the Middle Ages, the power of creation was understood to have rested directly with women, or between women and the Gods/Goddesses. It seems likely that women in pre-industrial cultures all over the world have also made this association, thereby assuming full responsibility for conception and for preventing conception. One indication of how far removed contemporary women are from their essential nature in this regard is the response of anxiety and suspicion that the idea of mindbody birth control can generate. Many women find it frightening to consider assuming 100% control of fertility management without external devices or supports. We have forgotten how to trust ourselves with our own mindbody processes.

One of the elements of my own experience was the decision to assume full responsibility for birth control, leaving no part of this with my male partner or with any other external agency. In some ways, this seems to contradict feminist principles, yet it is more like the understanding of ancient cultures where God was a woman, and the feminine was regarded with a respect that is not present today.

When I look to the masculine to take responsibility for contraception, I am asking him to share the burden. This sounds right, as long as I am experiencing fertility management as a burden. It makes sense that we want to share a task, or even be relieved of it, when it is difficult and burdensome. If, however, we can experience birth control as an empowering connection with oneself, with Nature, with the Goddess in her many forms, then it is a different story. We can still share the intimacies and passions of love making, and the decisions about having children, but the process of engaging and managing the life-giving power can be embraced fully as a woman's task.

For Angela, a single mother in her late thirties, birth control had not been an issue for a number of years. When she met Mark, she was delighted to enter into a new relationship and they thought long and hard about whether this relationship would involve having a baby. Clearly deciding no, she began practising mindbody birth control. In the early stage of learning to claim full responsibility for birth control, Angela had the following dream: *She is travelling in Tasmania with her father. They are looking at a travel book which shows a picture of a red waterfall. The waterfall can also be seen from where they are standing. Angela is telling her father how much she wants to visit the waterfall. He is dismissive, saying that it is too much trouble. He does not want to go. She asks a few more times and finally gives up.*

For Angela, the red flowing river was clearly linked to the menstrual flow. It seemed close and accessible, but her father said it required crossing some water to reach it, and she was waiting for her father to agree to the crossing. At the time of this dream, she did become pregnant while practising mindbody birth control. Despite being clear that she wanted no more children, she was looking to the masculine for permission or support. She was shocked to discover this internal attitude of dependency on "father". In her daily life, she lived independently, supporting herself and her teenage children, and successfully working in a profession. In Australia, Tasmania , the *inverted triangle* shaped island *down south* is a colloquialism for the female genital area. Angela's dream was telling her that her "father" was in her feminine ground, and that she was deferring to his wishes.

Engaging a process like mindbody birth control brings us face to face with the internal ground of our relationship with the masculine and feminine principles as they have developed in our personal history and in the culture. Women are beginning to discover that claiming equality with men is not the same as claiming the strength and power of deep feminine wisdom. Of course women can achieve in traditionally male dominated areas, and the struggle to make this obvious has been important. Yet all too often this equality has just proved that women can do it like a man rather than truly bringing an experience of the basic ground of feminine power that was lost along with the equality sometime in the past.

Women have always been able to do something that men cannot do, something so fundamentally important that the very fact of this inequality has produced a terrible reaction. Men cannot give life through their bodies. This is so obvious that we miss the significance of it.

When European people were making all those figurines depicting the feminine in Nature, the Goddess Creatrix, there was a deep reverence for the life-giving power of the feminine. This attitude seems to have fostered an equalitarian way of life for thousands of years. There is no evidence that human society ever involved a matriarchy where the feminine dominated and men were subservient or disempowered. The advent of patriarchy (where the masculine dominates and women are subservient) is a relatively recent development and is closely related to the lack of respect for the life-giving power of the feminine.

The inability of men to give life through their bodies has produced a striving for power in other ways, and a determined effort to reduce the significance of women's life-giving power. This has been so effective that we forget the fundamental truth of Nature that it is women who are responsible for reproduction, women who are the life-givers. All of the other achievements in human experience rest on the simple fact that, at the most basic level of existence, women are responsible for life. It is significant that so much time and money has been spent developing in vitro fertilisation when there are homeless children desperately needing an opportunity at life. Whom does IVF serve?

One answer involves the personal stories of the childless people whose suffering is relieved through the discoveries in this area. Another answer involves the collective takeover of the life-giving power of the feminine by science and masculine principles; Zeus giving birth to Athena, fully grown and armed, from his head.

Zeus was the father God in ancient Greek mythology. His first wife was Metis (Wisdom) who "knew more things than all the gods and men put together".[49] When the old Gods and Goddesses told Zeus that any children he had with Metis would be more powerful and overthrow him, Zeus swallowed Metis and her unborn baby, taking for himself the wisdom of the Goddess and her life-giving power. He developed a terrible headache, and Athena emerged.

Truly her father's daughter, one of Athena's most significant acts was to support Orestes after he had murdered his mother. Orestes was the son of Clytemnestra and Agamemnon, a hero of the Trojan war. Assuming the absolute right of the father, Agamemnon sacrificed his daughter, Iphigenia, to ensure swift winds for the fleet sailing to conquer Troy. Clytemnestra was enraged when she discovered the murder, and she avenged her daughter's death by killing Agamemnon when he returned from war. Orestes then avenged his father's death by killing his mother. This tragedy became a raging debate as the Erinyes (The Angry Ones), the avenging Goddesses, hounded Orestes, and Apollo supported him. The matter was settled by the Areopagus, an ancient Athenian council presided over by Athena. She ruled for Orestes, claiming that there was no such thing as Mother-right. The implications of this ruling are that fathers can do as they will with their daughters, mothers have no right to object, and the avenging Goddesses were renamed the Eumenides (The Soothed Ones). This has been a part of our cultural heritage for the last 2000 years or so!

CHAPTER FIVE

WOMEN'S MYSTERIES

It is not surprising that a practice like mindbody birth control has been forgotten. There have been strong political, religious, and cultural forces throughout history that have worked against women assuming autonomy of any kind, let alone the fundamental power of reproductive autonomy.

While a search of the books on mythology and ancient religions reveals much emphasis on fertility, they say very little about birth control. Were ancient women as helpless to control conception as modern women would be without medical science and technology? I think not, although there are very few direct references that support this.

One reference comes from twelfth century China, where a group of Taoist adepts known as *The Immortal Sisters* practised their version of mindbody birth control. One of them wrote the following poem that a colleague found in a book about ancient healing methods for women by Jeanne Elizabeth Blum, who believes that Zhou Xuanjing's poetry was referring "to life, the feminine, to energy, and gestation".[50] Specifically, one particular poem describes the process of internal regulation of fertility.

> The secret of the receptive
> Must be sought in stillness;
> Within stillness there remains
> The potential for action.
> If you force empty sitting,
> Holding dead images in mind,
> The tiger runs, the dragon flies -
> How can the elixir be given?
> The pedestal of awareness
> Is steady as a boulder -
> Let others flourish or fall,
> In a thousand different states.
> The yang light originally
> Is the wish-fulfilling jewel;
> Here you take it in
> To crystallise the great restorative.
>
> My mind is like the autumn
> In the heartland of Chan;
> I earnestly sit in mental work
> From midnight and noon.
> Fish and dragons are lively;

While the waves are still -
There is just the moonlight remaining
In the eternal sky.

Light smoke and thin mist
Block the empty sky,
Leaving the spiritual brightness
No place to abide.
Hate and love, prosperity and decline,
All are sharp swords;
I am like a despoiled virgin -
How can you look for me?
Essence and life must first be studied

In the moon cave;
Capture the dragon, bind the tiger,
Do not delay.
If yang leaks out during its development,
How can the granule be preserved whole? [51]

Blum has explained that "moon Cave" was a colloquial expression for the womb or vagina, and that "the Dragon" was associated with fertility and "in essence to 'capture the Dragon' would be to control fertility". Similarly, to "bind the tiger" refers to arresting and dispersing energy at acupuncture points associated with contraception or therapeutic abortion.[52] These Taoist adepts practised mindbody birth control, assuming full responsibility for managing fertility through an internal process of stillness with the potential for action. What a beautiful description of feminine ground.

There is just the moon light remaining

In the eternal sky.

Despite occasional finds like this wonderful poem, there is a general lack of references to birth control in the historical literature. This could suggest that women did not have knowledge in this area. This lack of information can, however, be understood in different ways. It is likely that such information was truly part of women's mysteries, an inner knowing, or a secret teaching, that was seldom recorded. In oral traditions that predominated in many parts of Europe and Asia well into this century, women's business was conducted in secret with no written records.

In her book, *Sex and destiny: The politics of human fertility*, Germaine Greer opened the chapter on contraception with the following words;

> (We) would gladly accept (family planning) provided it:
> - not interfere with our working;
> - not do us permanent harm;
> - not be against our religion;
> - be free or nearly so;
> - have a woman to examine us and to teach us what to do and how to do it
> - *remain a secret between her and us.*
>
> Women's Meeting, Central Javan Village, 1977.[53]
>
> [emphasis added]

The importance of secrecy in female mysteries is well known. In his book on the Great Mother, Eric Neumann noted that the primordial female mysteries became cults which "were kept secret by the women".[54] He also believed that these mysteries included the original secrets of feminine initiation as well as rules governing sexual intercourse and methods of preventing conception.

As well as being kept secret, it may also be that much of the information about early birth control practices has been lost. The remarkable efficiency of early Christians in destroying ancient written texts and images has been well documented[55], and knowledge preserved via an oral tradition is particularly vulnerable to religious and political purges. Jeanne Achterberg[56] has vividly demonstrated this in her historical account of the role of women in the Western healing tradition. So much has been lost or forgotten.

My own paternal grandmother could not read or write and could, therefore, only pass on her wisdom, learned from the elders in a small village in the south of Italy, by speaking. As she spoke no English and I spoke no Italian, I received no direct transmission of this wisdom. My father tells of how the women would meet in the village church on Christmas Eve to do women's business. As there were no men allowed, he does not know what happened. Of course I also cannot say what happened in the church at midnight, but my guess is that it was more Pagan than Christian, and that it had been happening for a very long time. But unless there is someone who can listen, these and other secrets can be lost in the space of one or two generations.

Celebrating the Wise Blood

The most basic way we know that we are not pregnant is when we menstruate. This cyclical bleeding is the Goddess's covenant with women since the beginning of time. Rather than celebrating this connection with the feminine mysteries, we tend to distance ourselves from this messy, inconvenient thing that happens at "that time of the month". Our menstrual blood signals our relationship with the life-giving power of the feminine, and it demonstrates our control over fertility each month when we bleed.

Moon diary

One way to attend to your body experience and deepen the conscious mindbody relationship is to keep a menstrual/ moon diary for 3 or 4 cycles. The idea is to note the moon phase every night and write a few words or draw an image about your, your physical state, and your experiences for that day. You can draw the moon phase from observing the moon in the night sky or from a moon calendar which is available from most bookshops. These calendars can be helpful for cloudy nights or when you lose track of the moon cycle.

The moon has been the focus of rituals and honouring throughout time. People meeting in the light of the full moon or the shadows of the dark moon have celebrated the cycles and changes, the eternal return. The cycles of the moon have long been associated with the menstrual cycle,

linking the functions of the womb with the sacred feminine principle.

Remember to note when you are menstruating and any other changes such as ovulation. The purpose of this is not contraception via moon cycles, although this is a practice used effectively by many women. The purpose of the Moon Diary is to train your attention to notice rhythms and cycles, the changes and shifts in the body and in your mood as you cycle through each month.

You may want to draw or use colours in your moon diary so choose a book that gives you room to experiment. The experience of actually going outside and finding the moon can also remind you of your connection to rhythms and cycles of Nature and the ancient feminine, something that is easily lost in modern life.

The practice of mindbody birth control involves welcoming the monthly bleeding. This is also a time when you can become familiar with the body sensations of shedding the lining of the uterus, one of the body sensing visualisations I used in my practice of mindbody birth control. I encouraged and invited the bleeding, imagining the body sense and mood state of menstruation, intensifying this inner process as my period became due each month.

One legacy of the loss of women's ways is that the wise blood has become "the curse" and is often greeted with less than enthusiasm. When we are regulating conception from within, the onset of menstruation is a much welcome sign of success. In ancient times, women in some cultures used sea sponges to absorb the blood similar to the way a modern woman uses a tampon. These women were closer to the experience of bleeding as the sponge was removed, rinsed in cold water, and reinserted. The blood could be poured on the earth in honour of the Great Mother and was not greeted with aversion or revulsion. It was welcomed as a sign of the relationship between woman and the goddess. *The Wise Wound*, an excellent book by Penelope Shuttle and Peter Redgrove[57], explores the historical and cultural legacy of menstrual taboos and repression.

Getting blood on your hands

Many women have returned to more natural ways of managing the bleeding by using pure cotton tampons, washable pads, and sea sponges to absorb the blood. When we have hands on contact with the wise blood we are brought closer to our relationship with the rhythms and cycles of Nature, of the Goddess.

Consider using a washable pad or sea sponge, rinsing them in cold water in a bowl, and using it to water your garden or house plants.

You may also like to make a painting using menstrual blood. This is a powerful way to bring this hidden process out of the dark.

Even if these hands on experiences do not appeal to you, you can consciously welcome your monthly bleeding by spending some quiet time lighting a candle to the Goddess and acknowledging her presence in your life. It is said that

during menstruation the veils between the worlds are thinner so that a woman has access to mysteries not usually available.

In ancient times, and in many pre-industrial cultures, women took time out every month during menstruation. This was women's time, free of the normal everyday demands of family and community, time for rest, ritual and renewal. When I think of this, I sometimes wonder if it was women who invented the menstrual taboo, after all, and that its original purpose has become degraded over the centuries!

Anita Diamant begins her novel, *The Red Tent*, with a powerful statement about mothers and daughters,

> We have been lost to each other for so long. My name means nothing to you. My memory is dust. This is not your fault or mine. The chain connecting mother to daughter was broken and the word passed to the keeping of men, who had no way of knowing.[58]

She writes of the mothers and the grandmothers before them, who have so much to tell, so much we need to hear. I have found that the grandmothers are not far away when we make the time to attend.

Birth Control before the Pill

There was effective birth control before the Pill.

This takes many different forms in different times and places of human history. One common element is that women have usually placed less emphasis on preventing conception before the event and more on post-conceptive methods that bring on menstruation. This difference between pre and post conceptive birth control seems to reflect a difference in male and female approaches to contraception. Basically, the distinction is between prevention of pregnancy and induction of menstruation.[59]

It seems that, historically, women have linked prevention of conception with menstrual regulation. It is relatively recent development to think of prevention of pregnancy as involving repeated precautionary steps taken before intercourse to prevent something that may or may not occur. In other words, contraception does not need to focus on whether the sperm connects with the egg; it can be about whether or not the possibly fertilised egg would be welcome in the womb, or whether the spirit of the child would be invited to enter.

In my mindbody birth control practice, I told my uterus "No" to implantation. This involved an inner process of sensing the ovaries and fallopian tubes and uterus and repeating "No baby" while imagining and sensing a downward movement, and imagining the uterine lining falling away and shedding completely. This practice could happen after fertilisation may have occurred and did not involve anxiety about whether or not sperm and egg met. Whether or not I conceived depended upon whether or not I gave the fertilised egg a home in my womb. I could say "No" to implantation.

For some other women, the stop is at the point of sperm and egg meeting, or the point of the spirit of the child entering, and they have developed their own practices around this.

Paula is 38 years old and works in the area of healing. In her work with women, she has discovered that there are many mysterious ways in which healing occurs. She describes a time when she found herself pregnant with her fifth child, and had made the commitment to have an abortion;

> . . . that was definitely what I was going to do and it was a very short amount of time, maybe a day or so after that . . . I just let go and I had the bleeding . . . I was able to let go of the baby and choose to do this at ten weeks.

Paula had an experience of something that all the women practising some form of mindbody birth control report: the certainty that the decision is ours, or ours in negotiation with the Goddess or other force we experience as responsible for the life-giving power of the feminine. We are not passive in the process.

When women have an experience of power and control in fertility management, the enormous tension around intercourse no longer exists because the process of conception and implantation can be interrupted as easily after intercourse as before.

Once again, it may seem that this change has already occurred with modern contraceptive methods. Women are no longer held hostage to unwanted pregnancy and can experience greater sexual freedom, but the focus of conventional birth control is still the prevention of something that having sex can make happen. The man can still get the woman pregnant if the condom breaks or she forgets to take the Pill.

This directly addresses the issue of women's autonomy in birth control: If we are concerned about preventing something that can just happen to us, we place undue emphasis on the masculine role in birth control.

Of course I respect the role of the man in actually making a baby, but I believe the territory of birth control is different. It is the woman's mindbody system that must support the process of conception and implantation, or not.

If I am to assume total responsibility for whether or not I become pregnant, I must reclaim my sense of authority from any other forces that can affect my decision. What mindbody birth control does is shift the emphasis from the moment of intercourse to the woman's internal relationship with her fertility.

When a woman is managing fertility from this internal ground, no amount of intercourse will get her pregnant.

This is a radical notion, as it challenges the idea that women are passive agents who need to protect themselves from being acted upon by something from outside them. The fact that medical science has provided a variety of protections against conceiving does not alter the basic belief of being acted upon. With mindbody birth control, women are active agents who can choose how to respond to the interaction with outside forces.

Many women would claim to be active agents in their dealings with the world, yet at a very fundamental level, they are still operating as if they are passive in relation to conceiving (it is still seen as something that can happen *to* them). This has major implications for true choice and empowerment: When a woman feels as if conception can just happen to her, she is still accepting the rulings of a father God who has decreed that she must be ruled over by her "husband". This must translate into how she experiences herself in the world.

The experience of reclaiming women's wisdom, mysteries and power is, therefore, fundamentally entwined with reclaiming reproductive autonomy. When we take this task seriously, we expose the underpinnings of the patriarchal power base that, for all the shifts that have happened in women's rights, is still pervading our lives.

After all, how did the current reality come to be? Who says that women cannot determine internally, easily and naturally, whether or not sperm meets egg, whether or not a fertilised egg receives a home in the womb, or whether or not the spirit of a child is invited to enter?

Consider the political, religious and cultural implications of questioning this one accepted "fact".

If a woman knows that the act of sex is not what determines whether or not she becomes pregnant, the balance of power in procreation shifts from masculine to feminine. If what fundamentally and actually determines whether or not you become pregnant is solely your decision whether or not to support the process, the whole relationship with reproduction changes. And when the relationship with reproduction changes, the relationship with the world changes.

When women reclaim the life-giving power, and men recognise this, we can also reclaim our reverence for the Goddess and for Nature. Historically, it is this reverence that allows us to live in an equalitarian way without the horrific abuses and deprivation experienced by so many women and children in the world today.

All of this raises questions about what makes us think and act the way we do. The information in this chapter suggests that there is a bigger picture, a bigger story which, once seen and heard, has the power to change the way we think about and practice birth control. And how we think about and practice living.

Most importantly, the information in the previous pages has probably stirred certain responses for you as you read of the historical events that have led to our current attitudes and beliefs. I suggest again that you journal your responses, paying particular attention to dreams (both night dreams and daydreams).

This material has called forth many powerful internal responses for women, responses that are the beginning of reclaiming what has been lost over the ages.

It is important to draw or paint or use clay to sculpt any images that arise for you, to dance and move, as well as writing about your experiences. If these practices are unfamiliar to you, begin with something simple like a journal with unlined pages and a packet of felt-tipped pens. You can write down day dreams, nighttime dreams, thoughts and daily events, and begin to draw or add colour to your words. Your personal responses are the basic ground of your becoming.

It can also be helpful to meet with other women to discuss the material and your responses. In Part III, I have included my own dreams and journal entries from the time of researching and writing about mindbody birth control. Jungian analyst, Marion Woodman, calls this sort of collection of personal material a "soul story"[60].

You can come to know your own soul story through attending to dreams, body sensations, self-reflective writing, and images. It was the profound impact of these sort of personal experiences that took my work from a very personal experience to an academic paper to a calling that has demanded expression in this book.

The ancient feminine mysteries are alive and well in our bodies, in our psyches, often just waiting for us to listen with other ears and see with other eyes.

I invite you to consider which myths will be the determining stories of your life. Now that you know how myth works to pattern your perceptions and beliefs, you can choose more consciously. Take some time to remember and record the stories from the culture, from your family, from your education, the stories that have consciously or unconsciously patterned your experience of fertility management.

What are your beliefs about birth control? What is your guiding story, your myth? What are your beliefs about claiming power and autonomy?

CHAPTER SIX

LIVING MYTHS

EXERCISES FOR DEVELOPING A PERSONAL MYTHOLOGY

Throughout time, people have explained their experience of the world through stories. These stories can be collective, familial, and personal. Even while whole tribes and cultures have their own mythologies, family groups and individuals also tell stories consciously and unconsciously that make sense of and define their world. Dreaming can also be understood as one way the unconscious tells stories that have meaning, personally and collectively.

Psychology has recognised the impact of the personal stories that arise out of childhood experiences, calling them scripts, schemas or defining beliefs. The consensus about these stories is that while they made sense in the context in which they developed, they usually become outdated as the person grows, becoming less relevant and even destructive in adult life. There are also scripts, schemas and beliefs that are passed down through the generations of a family, sometimes taking the form of a "curse" that takes its toll on successive generations. And, of course, there are the scripts, schemas and beliefs of the culture as a whole.

Just as it is possible to take a critical look at the myths of ancient Greece, recognising the patriarchal bias in many of the stories, it is also possible to examine cultural, family and personal myths to reveal underlying beliefs and "truths". If these so-called truths are not questioned, they can shape our lives without our permission.

By examining the myths that make up your life, you will reveal existing patterns and be able to develop new myths by which to live.

It is important to begin with the stories as they are rather than simply constructing an idealistic tale of how things would be in a perfect world. To understand the forces at work in your life, begin with the stories of your culture, your family and your own inner world.

This is an opportunity to examine the myths by which you are currently living. From where do they come? Do they adequately explain all of who you know yourself to be? Or do they require you to agree to certain illusions like the people in the story of *The Emperor's New Clothes*?

Take some time to write the stories of your culture, your family and your own journey.

The cultural myth

Cultural myths or belief systems are the collective stories that become accepted as truth. The way in which the stories of the past are interpreted influences the experience of the present. There is, for example, a vast difference between history as we have known it and herstory as it is now being told.

In his exploration of the spiritual legacy of the ancient world, Peter Kingsley[61], has poetically and powerfully described the way in which "dramas of misinterpretation, of misuse and abuse" can fundamentally alter the way a culture develops. He convincingly argues that Western culture is shaped by a series of errors in understanding, some the result of deliberate distortions and some the result of laziness and ignorance and the passage of time.

You can explore cultural stories for meaning and value, truth and superstition, fact and fantasy as they relate to women's business, including birth control and women's reproductive experiences. The idea and practice of mindbody birth control involves a shift in cultural-historical patterns. The following exercise can be applied to any area of your life where there may also be a shift trying to happen.

Begin writing the cultural myth(s) with "Once upon a time . . ."

There are many source books for this exercise listed at the end of this chapter. You may want to read more widely before writing your own version. You may find yourself writing several alternate histories (herstories). It is interesting that the popular genre of fantasy literature is sometimes referred to in just this way, as "alternate histories". These fantastic stories invite a rearrangement of the accepted versions of the past that have formed the present. The intense interest in the *Lord of the Rings* movies indicates a fascination with alternative cultural-historical patterns (alternate histories).

If you were to write the story of the feminine principle in the Western world since ancient times, what sort of story would it be? Fairytale? Romance? Horror? Murder mystery?

There are many beliefs that have been woven into the fabric of our cultural heritage. It can be difficult to unravel the strands as we have become accustomed to the colours and textures of our way of life. Some of the strands discussed in the previous chapter profoundly affect birth control practices. They involve limiting beliefs like the following:

- the Pill is the first reliable method of birth control
- unplanned pregnancy is shameful
- menstruation is unpleasant and should be hidden
- things have always been the way they are now
- reproduction does not involve creativity
- Eve's "sin" brought evil into the world
- women are only worthwhile if they are slim
- we should have one solid identity
- experts know best
- the responsibility for birth control should be shared equally by men and women
- women's ability to create life in their bodies is not real creativity
- if it hasn't been proven by science, it's not true

- if we haven't heard of it (or seen it in writing), it doesn't exist

I invite you to explore these and other cultural beliefs for their influence on your capacity to claim power, choice and control in fertility management and in your life more generally.

The family myth

Most of us have heard stories of our family history, directly or indirectly. The direct stories are the anecdotes told about ancestors and the family's fortunes and misfortunes. The indirect stories are sensed when visiting relatives, looking at photographs, hearing the whispering in the walls of family homes.

One way to start writing your family myth is to hold these impressions in awareness and write the words "Once upon a time . . ." (*Once upon a time there was a family of money lenders . . .; Once upon a time there was a king and a queen and they had three daughters . . .*).

Frame the known and sensed history of the family in these fairytale terms, setting the stage for the story to unfold. In mythic terms who were your ancestors? Poor peasant folk eking out a living in harsh conditions? Wealthy merchants accumulating profits and acquiring land? Ordinary men and women yearning for something more?

Take some time over this first sentence, giving form to the essence of your family. What you write may not be literally true (not many of us are descended from kings and queens), but make it true in spirit.

Once this first description exists, the next step is to develop the plot. What are the conditions of their lives? What is happening at the time of the story? What are their main concerns and troubles? What do these people like? What is their relationship with the people around them? With God/Goddess? What are the beliefs that determine the way they live?

Once again, allow your imagination to develop the story from your sense of the family.

Author, Robertson Davies[62], beautifully describes how family characteristics are "bred in the bone", whether we like it or not.

When in doubt about what happens next in the story, take some time to be with your bones, noticing the sensations in your body and allowing images, memories, tales to arise from within your body knowing. Look back over dreams that involve family members or family homes. Consider the countries from which the families have come. Look for the clues that tell the true story of your family.

A modern day family myth that involves themes of power and tragedy can be found in the story of the American "royal" family, the Kennedys. While the story of one's own family may not seem as dramatic, it can be surprising what emerges as the tale unfolds. When we can examine our family patterns from this perspective, it is possible to understand some of the myths that are determining our life choices.

As you write this story you may become aware of some of the underlying beliefs that cut across your intention to practice mindbody birth control or make other changes in your life. Here are some of the limiting family beliefs women have encountered as they engaged this journey:

- Blood is thicker than water
- No one will love you like your family
- Girls should be seen and not heard
- You must obey your mother and father
- Mother and/or father know best
- The world is dangerous
- You can't trust strangers
- Our religion is the only true religion
- You owe everything to us

You may recognise some of these, or you may discover other restricting beliefs in your family system as you write the family story in mythic terms.

The personal myth

This story also begins with "Once upon a time . . ." and extends out of the cultural and family myths into the structure and dynamics of the individual psyche. Personal myth has been described as a life-line to the million-year-old man or woman in us all.

When I set myself the task of writing a personal myth about fifteen years ago, I found the story almost writing itself. It certainly did not come from a rational, cognitive place. It was not a long or especially complex story, yet it has continued to inform me and reflect the life path that I find myself walking. Writing about personal experience from the perspective of myth or fairytale allows for a stepping outside of reality as we have known it and makes it possible for other perspectives to enter.

The following is an example of a personal myth I wrote when I began my doctoral thesis on mindbody birth control.

Once there was a golden child, glowing with light, loving, creative, relating openly and fully to the world. One day this child was wandering in the bush, enjoying the smells of moist eucalyptus and the colours of the bush. So many shades of green, with the vividness of the occasional wild flower. There was a sense of wonder and endlessness.

Suddenly a serpent slithered out onto the path and, before the child could move, he was wrapped tight in the serpent's coils. This was no ordinary serpent; this was a very old, ancient power of evil. The serpent took the child to his cave and bound him in the darkest corner so he could see no light. Then he began to reach into the child's mind and heart and soul and to entrance him with evil, to replace joy with fear, love with hate, light with darkness, trust with betrayal, openness with possessiveness. And he nearly succeeded.

Except for a small spark of light which would not go
out. No matter what the serpent did, he could not
extinguish that last glimmer of light. He could have
killed the child, but that would have been an
admission of defeat because death comes to all sooner
or later, and it is not the same as turning light to dark.
Sometimes in his anger, he was tempted to kill the
child, but pride prevented him. He wanted to kill that
last spark of light; it became an obsession.

*Sometimes, not very often, someone who carried some
of the light would pass by the cave, on the path where
it went back into the hillside, or on the path far below
in the valley, and the child would stir in his trance of
darkness. The serpent was ever watchful for this, and
would strike at the passer-by, inflicting fear and
injury, or even death if the venom went deep enough.
Nothing was going to come between him and his
submission of the light in the child, which had come to
represent total dominion over all light.*

*Occasionally there chanced a wanderer who was
immune to the serpent's poison and then the child
stirred almost awake, and his agony was horrible. For
he could, in those moments, realise his peril and the
utter helplessness of his entrapment. He could not free
himself; all he could do was remain true to that last
spark of light. He knew then, for those moments, that
something must come from outside to free him. But he
could never imagine what. And as the wanderers
passed by, and the child sank back into the trance of*

darkness, he felt the overwhelming terror and rage of his helplessness.

How could anyone even know of his plight, let alone help him? All of those who passed by saw only a snake, vicious and deadly to be sure, but, nevertheless, only a snake, protecting its territory. Occasionally one or two wanderers caught a hint of evil, but passed it off with a shudder. How could the child ever be free?

One day, a woman came walking along the top path. A beautiful woman, wearing clothing of many layers of fine, transparent fabric. She moved so silently that the child did not stir and the serpent did not notice her coming.

She stood to the side of the mouth of the cave and as her fine, flowing garment moved with the breeze, the serpent noticed the gentle lifting and falling of the veils in the corner of his eye, and became entranced, his mind drifting back through time following the flowing tail of a golden fish.

And, as the veils of illusion closed around the serpent, the trance lifted from the child, who came slowly back from the deep, dark place where he had dwelt for so long. He awakened to darkness, and to quiet, and to the absence of menace.

It took some time for him to find the balance in that spaciousness. All he had known for a long time, all that was familiar, was suddenly absent, lifted off. Eventually, he dared to move. And, in moving, he remembered wandering in the bush, remembered being trapped by the serpent, and remembered the eternity entranced in his coils.

He moved past the serpent into the day, blinking in the light which pulsed as if alive. He noticed the lifelessness of the serpent and the movement of veils and, for a moment, glimpsed their meaning. That glimpse lent depth and texture to the light in which the child moved. From time to time, he chanced to see the movement of veils, reminding him of illusion and, from his own entrancement he knew the power of darkness.

As the years went by, he would walk along the path, savouring the play of light on the leaves, and remembering a long ago dream of a serpent and a cave. One day, he found his way back to the cave. There was a large coiled rock to one side of the entrance, and no sound from within. Finding courage, he ventured inside and was surprised to find it not very deep and relieved to find it completely deserted. As he left the cave, he glimpsed movement in the corner of his eye. He turned and there, caught in the branch of a bush, was a gossamer fine piece of fabric, a plaything of the breeze. Yet, how it enchanted him and awoke in him an unnameable yearning.

This story came quite spontaneously once I sat down to write, and there are many layers of meaning in it for me. For example, the coils of the serpent are like the constraints of conditioned thinking, binding me to certain beliefs and particular ways of perceiving and understanding. There is also Jung's commentary on the symbolism of the serpent[63], where he describes the brooding quality of introversion which is like the snake coiled around its own egg and threatening life with its poisonous bite. In this sense, the serpent in my personal myth reflects my tendency to introversion that could prevent me from bringing my work into the world by coiling around it endlessly. The feminine figure who appears to free the child is like the Goddess, releasing my creativity from the binding beliefs of my reptilian brain, primitive beliefs about survival and safety. The associations and connections go on and on . . .

Working with beliefs

I have worked with many people to develop their personal myth in this way as a part of the therapy process. The stories have been long and short, vividly illustrated, or written on scrap paper. Almost always, people have been surprised and delighted by what emerges as they engage this task. They discover underlying beliefs that limit their experience of themselves and the world, and they find ways to move beyond them.

In working with new behaviours and choices, you will encounter cultural, personal and family beliefs that disrupt your intention or even discourage you from starting. Some of these will not become evident until you challenge them by doing something differently. The following restricting beliefs have been recorded by women as they worked to develop mindbody birth control as a regular practice. They initially showed up as emotional responses, inner doubting or critical voices, thought patterns, and difficulties with engaging the various tasks. Through the exercises described in this book, women have been able to identify the more personal beliefs at work in their experience and reclaim choice and control.

These restricting beliefs cluster around particular areas of our experience. Each of these areas has been called a matrix as it is made up of an interwoven belief system. In the 1999 science fiction movie, *The Matrix*, Keanu Reeves as "Neo" is woken from an unconscious sleep in which he believed he was living autonomously but was really controlled by alien forces. Becoming aware of the underlying beliefs that shape our lives can be like waking up from a long sleep. Like Neo, we are asked to choose between falling back into forgetfulness or coming fully into awareness of the underlying forces that determine our lives. "If you take the blue pill," says Morpheus in *The Matrix*, "you wake up and believe whatever you want to believe. You take the red pill and you find out how deep the rabbit hole goes."

Which will you choose?

An image from the ancient mystery practice of alchemy shows an adept or seeker about to climb the "holy mountain", up the steps leading to the highest point, the goal of the inner work. Just near the seeker stands an alchemist pointing towards a rabbit disappearing down its hole. Like Neo, Alice, and the alchemical adept, we need to follow the rabbit on a mysterious journey where we learn that there are other ways of seeing and experiencing ourselves and the world. Like Inanna, we must turn our ear to the "Great Below".

There are many beliefs that would stop us following that rabbit. These beliefs apply to practicing mindbody birth control, regulating body weight, expressing a creative vision, developing a skill, realising a dream etc. etc.

Belief clusters or matrices in reproductive choice :

Self worth

- I'm useless
- I can't trust myself
- I can't look after myself in the world
- I'm bad if I disagree with mother/ father/ authority figure
- I am incapable
- I don't deserve to be my own person
- My body is bad
- My body is not worth caring for
- I hate being a woman
- I will never be able to do it
- I am inferior
- I will lose my identity
- If I don't know everything, what I'm doing is worthless
- I don't know what I'm doing
- I can't get it right
- I can't change
- I don't want to try because I know I'll fail

- I am not creative
- I am unlucky
- I am unmotivated
- I am unintelligent
- My mind is too cluttered to concentrate
- It's too hard

Lack of autonomy, power and choice

- Independence is bad
- I am not allowed to become who I really am
- I can't find my real self
- I can't be in control of myself
- I'm not allowed to control myself
- I have no control over my life
- I can't stand up for myself
- I can't do what I want
- Everyone knows more than I do about everything
- I must please others
- My needs are not important
- If I don't please others, they'll leave me
- I am not responsible for myself
- I don't have to finish what I start
- Without other people's love, I'm nothing
- I only do what certain others approve of
- When I'm on my own I can't take care of myself
- I can't fight for myself
- I can't think for myself
- I have to be helpless
- I can't support myself
- I can't organise my own life

- I can't make it on my own
- No one is there for me in an emergency
- What I do for myself can never be enough

Safety

- The world is dangerous
- I can be used sexually
- I can't protect myself
- My power is dangerous
- Women are not trustworthy
- It's not safe for me to feel
- Change is too scary
- I'm safe as long as I'm pleasing others
- Bad things will happen if I fail
- I am not safe
- I'm not safe in my body
- It's not safe to be connected to my body
- It's not safe to remember
- I will hurt myself

Fear of the sacred

- I don't deserve to connect with the Goddess
- The Goddess does not exist
- The Goddess is dangerous
- Nature is not safe

Shame

- My body is not my own
- I am shameful
- My ideas are shameful

Quite a list! And you can probably add to it as well. These beliefs limit our capacity to assume power, control and choice in our lives. The problem is that they can seem very convincing until we take the time to name them and find ways to reduce their power.

By exploring beliefs in mythic terms, you can begin to separate from them and discover alternative responses. *The Wayward Princess* is a mythic tale that tells of leaving a limiting belief system and engaging a journey of discovery.

Writing your personal myth

Set aside some time for writing your personal myth. Choose a specific topic, or a particular limiting belief or response to the idea of women's wisdom, or about your ability to access it. This is the starting point for your myth.

Seeding

This involves gathering information that seeds the story so that it grows from within your experience. Spend some time considering your topic, writing down all the conscious associations that come as you take some time to be with it. Use the following procedure:

Step 1. Draw a small circle in the middle of a blank piece of paper and write the topic in the circle. Allow any and all associations to form and write these around the circle like the spokes of a wheel. Find at least 8 words that come from the topic in a meaningful way for you.

Step 2. Write a whole sentence using just the words around the outside of the circle, adding connecting words like *when, if, the, and, so etc*. Just allow this sentence to form naturally, even if you are breaking the normal rules of grammar, and you are not sure of its meaning. This is one way the unconscious can tell us a story, just like when we dream.

The following example comes from an exploration of my Italian heritage. I put "Italy" in the centre and added the following words as associations:

Passion
Mona Lisa
Latin lovers
Good food
Opera
Mama
Dante
Colour
Alps
Vatican

Then I made a sentence using the associations and some connecting words:

When I long for passion, I remember the Mona Lisa and think of all the Latin lovers she must have had while eating good food and listening to opera even if her mama did not approve and Dante could see the colour of the Alps even if the Vatican couldn't.

Step 3. Now draw your sentence in pictures, following the sequence of the sentence. These can be very basic stick figures or child-like drawings to represent the words. The pictures need only have meaning for you, your connection to the words. Another person seeing them may not recognise the image or symbol in the same way. Be sure to keep them in the same order as the sentence.

Step 4. Hide the original word map and sentence and go for a walk, make a cup of tea or coffee, take a break. When you come back to the exercise, pretend you are seeing the "hieroglyphics" for the first time. Let them translate themselves to you into a new sentence. There is no right way or wrong way to translate the hieroglyphics you have drawn. Once again, just allow the unconscious to tell you a story from the pictures. This can be the starting point for a whole myth. Stay with the order of the pictures and add connecting word to bring your translation to life . . .

Step 5. Use the final sentence as the starting point for your myth. It may not make sense immediately, but it can lead to a story that emerges from the inside rather than being constructed from the outside.

Focusing on the body
Allow some quiet time for just noticing what is happening in your body when you consider your topic or belief, or the first sentence that has come from the hieroglyphic process. You may notice particular sensations or places in your body where these resonate. Rather than ignoring the body responses or trying to understand them in a rational way, you can learn a lot by just noticing the body experience and allowing any images or memories or internal voices/thoughts to come into awareness.

This process of allowing the body to reveal its wisdom is called "focusing", and has been developed as a therapeutic strategy.[64]

The practice of focusing has been central to my experience of this whole area, in the initial mindful attention to body processes, and in maintaining the practices. In the chapter on birth control, there are some examples of images and words that have come from women focusing on their experience of birth control. Learning to attend to your body in this way ensures that your story stays authentic to your experience.

Focusing script (adapted from Gendlin)

The following script for the focusing process can be taped so that you can do it easily. After several times you can simply enter into the internal state of attentiveness that allows images, symbols, words and memories to arise from your experience of the bodily felt sense. Hold the internal attention for several minutes, giving the mindbody system time to respond. It is important to write or draw any images that come so that the experience stays in conscious awareness. I'm sure you have had the experience of waking from a dream only to have it disappear from consciousness before you can write it down. Developing a relationship between our conscious awareness and the less conscious parts of ourselves takes practice.

Take some time to become quiet. Begin by noticing your breath as it moves in and out of your body. . .noticing the rise and fall of your chest as you breathe in and out.

Allowing your attention to settle in your body. . .noticing any sensations. There may be sensations of tightness or holding or sensations of warmth or comfort or other sorts of sensations. Just noticing whatever is present for you right now.

And you can notice if there is a particular issue you want to explore right now (always specify an issue such as a limiting belief or some other issue in your life). Holding this issue in awareness, and allowing your attention to remain in your body, notice where in your body there is a response to this. Attending now to the experience of this issue in your body. Noticing where you sense it and noticing the sensations in that part of your body. Allowing your attention to be with this experience of sensing this in the body.

You can also notice the feeling sense, like an aura of feeling around the sensations. This is the felt sense of this issue. Allowing your attention to stay with the felt sense without thinking about it in any of the usual ways. All you have to do is attend to the felt sense in the body . . .just noticing. And you can notice how it is possible for something to arise from the felt sense of its own accord . . .it may be an image . . .perhaps a word or a phrase . . .a memory . . .or something else that just comes into awareness of its own accord. All you need do is continue attending to the felt sense . . .just noticing. . .until there is a shift in the felt sense. And you can draw or write when this is appropriate for you.

Writing

The basic format of the personal myth is one suggested by David Feinstein and Stanley Krippner in their book on personal mythology. [65]

Part one

You are creating a story about someone in ancient times, a mythic or imaginary time and place who has a similar issue to yours. Begin with "Once upon a time . . .", describing the mythical or fairytale setting and the problem the character is facing in mythic terms.

- Describe where she/he lives, terrain and surroundings.
- How did this problem come about?
- Was it created in a relationship with another person, a prince/princess, friend, family member, or whoever?
- What created this problem in the character's life?
- Was a curse put on him/her? For what reason? By whom?
- Give an actual name and face to the demon or witch or wizard.

If you are working with a specific belief, imagine how this belief came about. What was happening in your character's life or in his/her family at the time that this belief formed?

Most of our beliefs made sense in the original context in which they formed. The problem is that they have become automatic and generalised to the whole of our lives. For example, people in times of war or persecution had good reason to believe that the world was a dangerous place and that standing out from the crowd was risky. This belief has survival value and tends to persist down through the generations until it becomes difficult for the descendants of these original survivors to claim independence or autonomy.

Part two

Describe how impossible it seems to defeat the demon/wizard/baddy and/or the problems it has caused. What methods have been tried with the issue/ belief/ response pattern in your life that have not worked to defeat or change it? Transpose these methods into mythic terms.

Staying with how impossible it seems/seemed to defeat the demon/witch/ dilemma is important as it helps prevent easy or glib solutions, demanding that you engage the problem until a solution emerges from within the story. Once again, check your body sense so that the story stays grounded in your experience.

At the end of this part of the myth, make a statement of the impasse: what is the specific obstacle the character is dealing with? How, specifically, do you feel knowing that nothing can be done to deal with it? Explore this mythically. Remember the impasse in my myth when the child could not free himself from the snake.

Part three

Begin with the words, "Then one day . . ."

Then one day what happened?

Let some solution to the impasse come to you. Give it time. If nothing arises in you to break the impasse, and no solution comes, then consider who or what might be able to deal with this demon/witch/problem. Imagine some heroic figure, animal or mythic creature and find out what happens when it meets your impasse. Let the story tell itself. You may be surprised and delighted as the story begins to unfold.

Allow time in which this story can come present. It may not emerge in one sitting or even ten sittings. As with other inner work with the imagination, what is required is a commitment to attending regularly to the process. It will emerge in its own time by allocating regular times for sitting with the unfolding story.

When your story is written, you can copy it into a special book and add pictures or decorate the pages. It can be as elaborate or as simple as you like. It is up to you. It's your story!

Readings for mythology

Cultural mythology

D Abram, 1996, The Spell of the Sensuous: Perception and Language in a More-Than-Human World, New York, Vintage Books.

L Blair, 1991, Rhythms of Vision: The Changing Patterns of Myth and Consciousness, Rochester, VT, Destiny Books.

A Diamant, 1998, The Red Tent, St Leonards, Australia, Allen & Unwin.

R Eisler, 1988, The Chalice and the Blade: Our History, Our

Future, San Francisco, Harper & Row.

J Gebser, 1991, The Ever Present Origin, Athens, OH, Ohio University Press.

M Gimbutas, 1989, The Language of the Goddess, New York, Harper & Row.

P Kingsley, 1999, In the Dark Places of Wisdom, Inverness, CA,
Golden Sufi Center,

G Lerner, 1986, The Creation of Patriarchy, New York, Oxford University Press.

L Shlain, 1998, The Alphabet Versus the Goddess: The Conflict Between Word and Image, New York, Viking Penguin.

M Sjoo & B Mor, 1987, The Great Cosmic Mother: Rediscovering the Religion of the Earth, San Francisco, Harper & Row.

M Stone, 1978, When God was a Woman, New York, Harcourt Brace Jovanovich.

WI Thompson, 1981, The Time Falling Bodies Take to Light: Mythology, Sexuality and the Origins of Culture, New York, St. Martin's Press.

EC Whitmont, 1982, Return of the Goddess, Guernsey, Channel Islands, Great Britain, The Guernsey Press.

JB Woolger & RJ Woolger, 1990, <u>The Goddess Within: A Guide to the Eternal Myths that Shape Women's Lives</u>, London, Rider.

Family mythology
AA Schützenberger, 1998, <u>The Ancestor Syndrome: Transgenerational Psychotherapy and the Hidden Links in the Family Tree</u>, New York, Routledge.

Personal mythology
DS Bond, 1993, <u>Living Myth: Personal Meaning as a Way of Life,</u> Boston, Shambhala Publications.

L Blair, 1991, <u>Rhythms of Vision: The Changing Patterns of Myth and Consciousness</u>, Rochester, VT, Destiny Books.

D Feinstein & S Krippner, 1997, <u>The Mythic Path: Discovering the Guiding Stories of Your Past - Creating a Vision for Your Future</u>, New York, JP Tarcher.

S Keen & A Valley-Fox, 1989, <u>Your Mythic Journey: Finding Meaning in Your Life Through Writing and Story Telling</u>, Los Angeles, JP Tarcher.

PART II.2

ANTHROPOLOGY

CHAPTER SEVEN

CYCLES OF MEANING
ANTHROPOLOGY AND WOMEN'S BUSINESS

Amy has practised mindbody birth control for many years. She is now fifty, with three grown children, and a successful career in education. She is very aware of the way in which our current consensus reality can shape our lives. She spoke with me about how

some tribal societies use the ideas of power, ancestral worship to contracept, and sometimes those of us in the Western worlds lose sight of such simple things.

While Amy is not an anthropologist, her thoughts reflect what researchers have found in pre-industrial cultures: safe, effective birth control that seems to involve a pact between women and the Gods or Goddesses of the tribe.

Anthropology studies people within the context of their cultures, revealing practices and beliefs that vary from place to place and from time to time. Most pre-industrial, traditional societies did not leave the process of forming and teaching the traditional beliefs of their culture to chance. They used ritual practices, elaborate preparation, and traditional interpretation of experience to ensure continuity. They must have known just how vulnerable to change the belief system of a culture can be.

Just as new information or experiences can be blended with the traditional to enrich a belief system, a break in the cycle can render it meaningless in a single generation. This is exactly what Anita Diamant describes in *The Red Tent*, when she says that

> the chain connecting mother to daughter was broken and the word passed to the keeping of men, who had no way of knowing.

The relative fragility of cultural systems is alarming when we consider the current rate of change in the world, and the disintegration of systems of meaning as cultures are irrevocably altered. This changeability does, however, confirm the idea that very different practices of birth control may well have existed before major cultural transitions such as the Inquisition or the Industrial Revolution.

We tend to assume a continuity in our cultural heritage that is not, in fact, the case. Things have not always been as they are now. There have been many shifts and changes that have brought us to where we are today.

Observations of other cultures can give us some idea of just how different things can be. There are cultures in which premarital sex was the norm, and where the young women rarely conceived until they were married. This may not seem unusual except that these young women did not use any obvious methods of birth control. For example, Bronislaw Malinowski[66], in his pioneering work in participant-observation of the Trobriand Islanders in the early 1900s, found that the Islanders did not make any connection between sexual intercourse and pregnancy. Pregnancy only occurred when a woman "invited the spirit of a child to enter her body". While the Trobrianders had strong taboos against pregnancy in unmarried girls, there were no taboos against premarital sex, and young people often lived together, having frequent sexual contact. Pregnancy rarely occurred in such relationships, and Malinowski could discover no forms of contraception, and abstinence was not practised. The Trobrianders simply believed that girls who did not invite the spirit of the child into their bodies would not conceive. The same girls, once married, invited the spirit of the child to enter and had no difficulty conceiving.

There are women who practice this method of birth control today. They describe a sense of the spirit of a child hovering during a time when they might conceive. A clear "No" to the spirit of the child usually sends it on its way. The following example shows what is possible when we start to think outside the usual ways.

Tanya, twenty-nine, with two young children, discovered that she was pregnant. Not yet ready for a third child, she was quite prepared to say "No" to giving this new child a home in her womb. She was, however, concerned about what would happen to the spirit of the child. I suggested that she think of someone she knew who was wanting to conceive. Her friend Wendy had one child, and she and her husband had been trying to conceive for six years. Tanya talked with Wendy about sending the spirit of this child to her. They agreed to light a candle each and, while Tanya directed the child to her, Wendy welcomed the spirit of the child into her womb. Tanya was delighted when she began bleeding the next day. Three weeks later, Wendy was delighted to test positive for pregnancy! This very welcome baby has since been born and the women share a joke about who the baby really looks like.

While it is very clear that Wendy's baby does have a father, the idea of paternal kinship was unknown to the Trobrianders. They just did not believe that a man contributed directly to making a baby. The generic term for kinship was "veiola", meaning kinship in the maternal line. Thus, while conception was preferred within marriage, there was apparently no direct connection made between sexual intercourse and conception. There was even a story of one young man who was convinced of the sexual faithfulness of his betrothed, but chose to marry someone else when his intended wife conceived a child at an "improper time" (and in his absence).[67]

What is significant about these observations of the Trobriand Islanders is the low incidence of conception amongst the unmarried, yet sexually active, girls. The only explanation of why these girls did not conceive at the normal rate of married women was that they had not "invited the spirit of a child to enter". In other words, their belief system interacted with their biological functions, so that they were, in fact, practising mindbody birth control.

The Trobrianders believed that the spirit of the child must be invited to enter for pregnancy to occur. In other words, there had to be an intention to conceive for pregnancy to occur. The women practising mindbody birth control all agree with this; the intention to not conceive must be clear for mindbody birth control to be effective.

Two of the women I interviewed used the word "ruthless" to describe their process of deciding to have no more children and to use mindbody birth control to ensure that they did not conceive. This certainty makes up the core of each woman's subjective experience of consciously regulating conception through a mindbody process.

One factor in the experience of reproductive autonomy is this capacity for ruthlessness. The idea of a particularly feminine ruthlessness is reflected in the following comment on woman's attitude to abortion;

> it is man who has evolved principles about the sacredness of life (which he very imperfectly lives up to) and women have passionately adopted them as their own. But principles are abstract ideas which are not, I believe, inherent in feminine psychology. Woman's basic instincts not concerned with the idea of life as such, but with the fact of life. The ruthlessness of nature which discards unwanted life is deeply ingrained in her make-up.[68]

This ruthlessness is one aspect of the feminine principle. Culturally, we have become accustomed to educated, intelligent women "taking it like a man"[69], and interpret competitiveness or the drive for success and achievement as feminine ruthlessness. Yet it may be that the feminine capacity for ruthlessness has a different flavour, and a different focus.

In terms of procreation, we are familiar with the ruthlessness of the mother in protecting her young, yet there is also a ruthlessness in refusing a foetus a place in which to grow, or a ruthless determination in protecting an egg from fertilisation, or a ruthlessness in saying no to the spirit of the child who wants to enter the womb.

Ruthlessly refusing to allow the spirit of the child to enter is one approach used by women practising mindbody birth control. Robyn, in her late thirties, and a mother of three teenagers, did not want any more children. She described "*the point of saying no to the being who might enter*" in her birth control practice. For Robyn, the biological process was not an important part of controlling conception, although she had a clear understanding of the reproductive cycle. Instead, she placed emphasis on her spiritual beliefs, describing at length the relevance of her spiritual practice to her experience of regulating conception;

> *The point of saying "No" is to the being who might enter. A prayer of asking that sexual sharing is a process of worship and if it is to do with my will, I do not wish to have a child . . .and ask to be protected from a child that does not really need to come.*

Amy, the 50 year old teacher who spoke of "power, spirit, and ancestral worship" in tribal cultures, described her practice of mindbody birth control as

> *. . . a thought perception rather than physical . . .very much out there. I'm sure there is something for people to connect with.*

Like the young women in the Trobriand Islands, an exchange took place "out there" that prevented the spirit of the child entering.

There are other cross-cultural examples of mindbody birth control. In the Muria culture of India[70] young people from five to seventeen lived separately from their parents in a "ghotul" dormitory. Within the ghotul, the teenagers had regular sexual relations, but only 4 percent of the young women became pregnant before marriage. Upon entering the ghotul, each girl took part in a ceremony in which the God of the ghotul was requested to keep her from becoming pregnant before marriage. Think about it: this was the only contraceptive measure used, yet they maintained a 96% success rate! The strong belief in the God of the ghotul allowed these girls to practice mindbody birth control.

Another story comes out of Africa. A field researcher with whom I corresponded described a local practice in which a woman would jump one way across a bush in order to conceive and the other way in order not to conceive.[71] This worked well unless the bush disappeared between visits . . .

It does seem that however we explain what we are doing, women can devise ways to manage fertility that truly offer reproductive autonomy. So much depends on the prevailing beliefs of the culture.

Take some time to consider these alternative belief systems. It can seem strange that some groups of people have not recognised the connection between sexual intercourse and pregnancy. This connection seems obvious to us because it has become part of the cultural reality. Malinowski, however, is quite clear that the tribal people he observed did not share our understanding of how babies are made.[72]

Remember, our knowledge of sexual reproduction is not innate. We are taught the information very much as the Muria children learned about the God of the ghotul and children in other cultures learn about the belief structures by which their elders make sense of the world. We need only listen to children in primary school wondering whether "kissing will make you pregnant", or whether a girl "gets pregnant through her belly button" to see this. Just over one hundred years ago, nineteenth century medicine was still debating theories of menstruation, with some physicians arguing that it was a pathology. The universal belief, with very few exceptions during the nineteenth century, was that conception occurred at menstruation. This belief persisted into the twentieth century and was only definitely disproved about 80 years ago[73]. The understanding of reproduction that we take for granted is a relatively recent discovery.

As you can see, there are many ways of thinking about conception and contraception. It could be that the idea of a symbolic creativity like that of the Trobriand Islanders is actually a higher order of thinking than our reliance on facts based on observations of the physical body.[74]

The biological role of the male in impregnation was often not given credence in ancient history and mythology. Women impregnated by means not involving mortal men have been described in myths from biblical times to more recent historical eras, and parthenogenesis (conception without male involvement) is also often described, with women becoming pregnant autonomously, without the fertilisation of man or God. In fact, spontaneous generation has been the subject of contemporary research, with somewhat astonishing results. Scientists have reported techniques of activation of eggs (silkworm, mouse, and bovine) toward parthenogenetic development.[75]

Ignorance about the causal relationship between sexual intercourse and pregnancy was also observed among traditional groups in New Guinea, and among the Arunta in Central Australia.[76] One contemporary researcher found that

> to the Aboriginal mind, the modern explanation of conception as the collision of sperm and egg is absurd. In their view, sperm may prepare the way for the entry of the child into the womb, but the spirit of the child appears in the father's dreams or inner awareness before conception.[77]

It seems that indigenous Australians also believed, and experienced, that a woman can be spiritually fertilised by coming into contact with a power related to a specific place:

> Every ancestor, while chanting his or her way across the land during the Dreamtime, also deposited a trail of "spirit children" along the line of his footsteps. These "life cells" are children not yet born: they lie in a kind of potential state in the ground, waiting. While sexual intercourse between a man and a woman is thought, by traditional Aboriginal persons, to prepare the woman for conception, the actual conception is assumed to occur much later, when the already pregnant woman is out on her daily rounds gathering roots and edible grubs, and she happens to step upon (or even near) a song couplet. The "spirit child" lying beneath the ground at that spot slips up into her at that moment.[78]

This magical story of conception takes baby making out of the purely physical, inviting us to think beyond what we have taken for granted. Regardless of which story we believe, women across cultures have been using their own idiosyncratic methods to prevent pregnancy. The Trobriand Islanders, the Muria and Australian Aboriginal people, would not have described mindbody birth control as I have. A strongly held belief or experience of the natural and supernatural worlds made conception impossible under certain conditions; for them the process was operating out of consciousness. The people of these cultures simply did not believe that pregnancy could occur under certain conditions, and, in the majority of cases, it did not. These ideas are important because they invite us to think beyond what we know as "truth", challenging our conditioned beliefs and suggesting new possibilities.

While I certainly have no argument with the embryology of biological science or with the role of the masculine in conception, it is intriguing to imagine other ways of perceiving reality and discovering what then becomes possible. Imagine what can happen when we loosen the bindings of our conditioned perception . . .

Anthropologist, Margaret Mead[79], said this:

> Behind all of these age-old devices (contraception, abortion, infanticide) there lies a subtler factor, a willingness or an unwillingness to breed that is deeply imbedded in the character structure of both men and women. How these relative willingnesses and unwillingnesses function, at what point in the reproductive process blocks are introduced, we still do not know, but the evidence leaves little doubt that they are there.

I would have liked the opportunity to tell Margaret Mead about my experience of mindbody birth control, and to hear what associations she might form with her observations of pre-industrial cultures.

She has said that

> It is possible that we may some day evolve a culture in which there will be such a good communication

within each paired relationship that no other control will be needed than the female's own natural monthly rhythm of fertility.[80]

I would add that it is the good communication within the woman's mindbody system (the paired relationship of body and mind) that makes this natural fertility management possible.

In contemporary developed cultures, we need to begin by developing some freedom from the conditioned expectations of our cultural learning. We also need to learn to recognise the conflicting "willingness" and "unwillingness" in our own systems.

The understanding from depth psychology is that there are unconscious parts of us that often want something different from our conscious intention. We all know the experience of deciding to diet or change our behaviour in some way, only to find another impulse taking over before the day is out. This internal conflict can arise in relation to any decision to change behaviour and is explored further in Part III.

Developing you own rituals

Imagine that you have grown up in a culture like the Trobriand Islands, or an imaginary place where the belief system support sexual freedom and your right to manage fertility through some sort of ritual process.

What would your fertility management ritual be? Would it involve a God or Goddess or some other deity?

Write this as a story, another alternate herstory. Allow the unconscious to begin informing you of how mindbody birth control can work for you. What are the elements of this for you? It may be a daily practice, or something that you only do on the full moon, or when your menstruation is due. It may be something elaborate or something simple. Take some time to find your relationship with the deep feminine mysteries that support this magical way of experiencing yourself.

CHAPTER EIGHT

ENVY:
WANTING WHAT WE DON'T HAVE

Male envy

Cross-cultural studies have revealed the extent of male jealousy of women's procreative powers. As in mythology and our own history, this jealousy works to diminish respect for the functions of the female body and to reduce women's access to the age-old wisdom of the grandmothers.

It has been recognised that the restrictive attitudes imposed on women during menstruation and childbirth arise from fear and envy of the female body and life-giving power.[81] There is even a name for it, "vagina envy"[82], a term that describes an envy and fascination with female breasts and lactation, as well as with menstruation, pregnancy and childbirth.

It is extraordinary to consider just how familiar the term "penis envy" is in everyday language, while the term "vagina envy" can only be found in dusty text books.

It has been suggested by psychoanalytic theorists that men want to create objects of value from within their bodies as women do. It is their disappointment in their inability to create human beings that has led them to intellectual creation, and that

> woman envy on the part of the man . . .is psychogenetically older and therefore more fundamental than penis envy . . .is not the tremendous strength in men of the impulse to creative works in every field precisely due to their feeling of playing a relatively small part in the creation of living things which consistently impels them to an overcompensation in achievement? [83]

In many cultures, the men perform rituals such as male genital mutilations and their associated ceremonies to strengthen their identification with the life-giving power of the feminine. These practices are a graphic example of a power struggle that has become much less visible in "civilised" society. Less visible, but no less potent, and even more destructive.

When men are mutilating themselves to acquire some of the power of women's reproductive experience, at least they are openly acknowledging the central importance of the life-giving capacity of the feminine. The same struggle continues in the modern world, but it is disguised as something else, such as reproductive and genetic engineering, or feminist victories that have women "talking it like a man", or the obsession with body image that so diminishes women. Whatever we call it, the effect in modern culture is to reduce the intrinsic value and sacredness of the life-giving power of the feminine.

In pre-industrial cultures, there are many rites and ceremonies that symbolise the wish of men for female sex characteristics and functions. The subincised penis is understood to symbolise all that is essential to the process of reproduction via the feminine. The men from one Aboriginal tribe, where subincision is performed, knew that the object of the sacred rituals (fertility and everything connected with it) belonged to the women, but that it was possible for them to steal these[84]. This is also reflected in the practice of couvade which is still seen today. Couvade is an experience in which fathers or men about to become fathers, ritually go through the motions of labour and childbirth as their partners are experiencing them.

This fascination and identification with "women's business" takes many forms. The Mundurucu people of Brazil believed that the gender that controls the musical instruments also controls the society. Their story was that the women originally controlled the instruments and, although men took control from them, women were constantly attempting to retrieve them.[85]

Similarly, Margaret Mead[86] has described South Seas cultures in which men acquired the mystery of guarding the secrets of life via the playing of a sacred flute. In this case, the central life of the tribe revolved around the making, learning, and ritual playing of the flute, tasks from which women were excluded. In this tribe which revered fertility, the men had found a way to compensate for being excluded from the activities of reproduction. In the Iatmul culture of New Guinea, the initiatory myths tell how it was the women who discovered the sacred noise-making objects and "decided" to give them to the men. The story goes that the women even asked the men to kill them so that the secret could remain with the men forever.[87] I suspect that story was written by a man!

There is a contemporary version of acquiring the "sacred noise making objects" (read "life-giving power" for "sacred noise-making objects"). The story is about reproductive technology. Even while reproductive technologies have been developed to relieve the suffering of childlessness, they are also used to develop applications that can replace the life-giving functions of the feminine. There are many writers and researchers who recognise how these technologies can be used to gain control over the life-giving power of women's bodies.[88]

There are also many cultural practices that protect sacred objects from "female pollution". The widely held belief in female pollution is based on the perception that menstrual blood is somehow contaminating and must be avoided by males at all costs. As we have seen, menstrual avoidance practices can also be explained in terms of male concerns about power and control. As so many tribal practices demonstrate, underneath the disgust and avoidance is the desire to take something back from the females. The Mundurucu men openly admit that the structural segregation and fear of women during menstruation are mechanisms by which the men preserved their dominance over women.

This makes sense of the menstrual taboos practised throughout history and across cultures: they are a determined effort to wrest power from women, especially the fundamental power to create new life. Menstruation is clearly a sign that a woman is not pregnant, that the power of creating life is hers. It is also a reminder that the feminine power of creation is inaccessible to the male in any direct way. From this perspective, male ambivalence toward menstruation, and the practice of menstrual taboos, actually reflect women's exalted state and their real power as propagators of the species.[89] Once this is recognised, the next step is to reclaim the power and dignity that has been lost.

This is not just something that affects women in pre-industrial cultures or orthodox communities. Several surveys of contemporary attitudes and practices surrounding menarche, menstruation, pregnancy, and the post-partum period, indicate a continuing belief in the polluting quality of female sexuality and fertility.[90] These attitudes are profoundly destructive of our ability to develop conscious relationship with our bodies, our sexuality, and our reproductive practices.

Male envy of women's life-giving power is a compelling motive for the historical takeover of the power and mystery of the feminine role in procreation during the transition from matrifocal to patriarchal values over the last 5000 years. This transition has had a catastrophic effect on women's ability to regulate the rhythms and cycles of their own bodies and to authentically use and develop birth control practices based on the feminine principle. The fact that more women do not know about mindbody birth control can be traced to what was lost during this time. We have been made ashamed of our bodies, especially our reproductive capacity, and we have turned away from our heritage as daughters of the Goddess. Shame is a device for controlling the flow of the red river that symbolises women's reproductive magic. Once you recognise this, you can begin to regain choice and control, the fundamental steps in claiming true reproductive autonomy.

Women and envy

Envy is not, of course, the exclusive province of the masculine. While men are envying women's life-giving power, women are busy envying all sorts of things about each other. It is an insidious element in many friendships and family relationships.

Working with envy

List the ways in which you have encountered envy in your life, both collectively and personally. You may not have thought about your experience in this way before. Many women say that they just felt hurt, shamed or diminished by an experience without recognising the envious attack.

Envy is insidious as it can appear in a voice tone, facial expression, or the "yes, but" tacked onto the end of a compliment. It can appear in patronising comments, or it can be disguised as helpfulness.

When one of Sandra's old friends visited each new place she lived in, the friend would begin by admiring the view or the location or the lay-out but finish by making an aside such as, "It's such a pity you still have that old couch" or

"I wonder why they used that colour there". These sort of comments take the shine off the experience and leave the person on the receiving end diminished.

Envy can also show up as comments about appearance: "You look great in that. Isn't it a shame that top didn't come in a bigger size."

Whenever you come away from an interaction feeling somehow diminished or shamed, there is a good chance that you have been on the receiving end of an (often unconscious) envious attack.

Learning to recognise envy when it appears is one way to counter its effects. There is a power in naming.

The evil eye

In cultures in Southern Europe, the Middle East, and Africa, people believe in the power of the "evil eye". The evil eye is brought upon someone by human envy or anger, and is averted through ritual practices to protect the family from envious attack, either from other people or from the Gods. The ritual with which I am most familiar is the one my Italian grandmother used.

Banishing the evil eye

To perform this ritual you will need a bowl of water, some olive oil in a shallow dish, salt, two needles, and a pair of scissors.

Place the bowl of water on a table or the floor near a lighted candle. Think of the situation or symptom that concerns you (a headache, body pain or sudden illness is often associated with envious attack in Italian tradition).

One at a time, allow 3 drops of olive oil to drip from the end of your finger into the water. As close as possible allow the drops to fall in the same place. If the drops join together, envy is not present. If the drops stay separate or join up and spread over the surface, envy is present.

In this case, take the two needles and put the point of one through the eye of the other and say some words to banish the envy (Raven Grimassi[91] in his book on Italian witchcraft suggests the following: *Occhi e contro e perticelli agli occhi, crepa la invida e schiattono gli occhi -- Eyes against eyes and the holes of eyes, envy cracks and eyes burst.*)

Drop the needles into the bowl through the oil and sprinkle three pinches of salt into the water.

Stab the scissors through the oil drops three times and cut three times in the space above the bowl. The envious attack is cleared.

You can use your own words to cleanse the envy from your system. This may involve naming the envious attack and refusing it a home, or making a general statement about being rid of it. If you are concerned about sending the envy back out into the world, you can imagine that a candle flame can burn up any residue

Envy is also something we can feel for others, especially when we are bombarded with images of beautiful bodies, expensive clothes, exotic holidays, and happy couples. One way to work with your own experience of envy is to recognise that **envy is actually an expression of longing.**

When we desire to have something or experience something, we often come up against the sort of beliefs and internal messages listed in the last chapter. Believing I am unworthy of the experience or unable to get what I want leaves me longing for what I desire but powerless to have it. At least the envy keeps the longing alive.

When we can recognise the longing and begin to use our imagination to explore it, our envy can be transformed into a potential for action on our own behalf.

Envy and imagination

Take some time to list the people you envy. Identify the expressions of longing in your envy. What is it that they have that you are desiring or wanting to bring into your life? What cuts across you having this or bringing it about? Is there a belief or internal message that stops you? Identify this limiting aspect. Use some of the mindfulness and attention exercises from this book to explore this.

Begin to imagine what needs to happen for these longings to move you to take action in your life. What would it be like to have the desired object or experience? How would you be different? If someone who knows you well saw you walking down the street after attaining or achieving your desire, what would they notice? Would you be walking differently? Perhaps you would be smiling? Step into the picture of yourself as having already satisfied your longing.

Write a story or poem about your desire. An exercise I have shared with women in groups is writing a sexual fantasy and sharing it in the group. Everyone is surprised and delighted by the energy that becomes accessible when we recognise our longing and use imagination to bring it to life.

And, of course, it can lead to new behaviours and experiences.

CHAPTER NINE

AESTHETICS: PLEASING YOURSELF

The word "aesthetics" comes from the Greek for perceiving. In the English language, we tend to use the word to refer to an appreciation of beautiful things. I use the word here to explore how women feel about birth control. Does it seem beautiful to them? Does it have a quality that brings pleasure to the senses or the mind?

On the contrary.

It has been suggested by one Jungian analyst that

> to a great many women contraceptives, though accepted intellectually, are still unaesthetic, and to a deep basic feminine morality they are wholly unacceptable.[92]

What is this deep, basic feminine morality?

Basic feminine morality is linked to the rhythms and cycles of Nature, to the experience of change and renewal that is so clearly reflected in a woman's menstrual cycle. It involves an appreciation of time:

The time it takes for one whole cycle of the moon (remember that women were the first time keepers, with sticks marked for the phases of the moon and the menstrual cycle).

The time it takes to grow a baby from the first spark of life to the fully formed child ready to be born.

The time it takes to give birth.

The time it takes for a child to grow into an adult.

Feminine morality is about working with Nature, with the natural rhythms and cycles.

It could be argued that birth control has to work against Nature; in order to prevent pregnancy, the natural process of conception has to be interrupted. Of course, that is completely true. There is, however, a vast difference between using a synthetic hormone that *acts on* the mindbody system, and engaging a process that *works with* the mindbody system to bring about a shift that is ecologically sound. When something is ecologically sound, all the parts of the system are in agreement; any changes that occur are harmonious throughout the whole system and nothing is being forced or suppressed in an absolute way.

When we use a synthetic hormone or chemical that is designed for a specific purpose, we are introducing something into our system that cannot be used by the body in any other way. On the other hand, the naturally occurring neuro-chemicals and hormones in the body can be changed and redirected by the mindbody system to maintain balance and harmony. One of the serious consequences of the widespread use of oestrogen-based oral contraceptives is that the oestrogen/progesterone balance in women's bodies has been undermined.[93] The synthetic hormones take up space that would otherwise be used by the naturally occurring body hormones. When this happens, the natural levels fall, and the body's ability to continue producing the natural hormones is affected.

Even when a woman does not have this biochemical knowledge, she may still find the contraceptive Pill "unaesthetic".

Our deep basic feminine morality is supported by a reverence for the life-giving power of the feminine. When we reconnect with the ancient feminine principles that underlie reproduction, we rediscover the forgotten mysteries of women's ways that offer true reproductive autonomy. We reclaim power, control and choice.

As we have seen in the stories from mythology and anthropology, the most important aspects of birth control involve these issues of power and control, and the prevailing beliefs about how reproduction works. Overwhelmingly, I have found that women today express strong concerns about power and control in their experience of contraception. Earlier, I quoted Jane who said that

> . . .*either the Pill was not helping or it was one more thing where I felt controlled.*

This experience of feeling controlled can arise in relation to all aspects of fertility. In my home state of Victoria, Australia, for example, the statistics for caesarian birth indicate a disturbing degree of taking over by the medical profession (23% in 1999-2000 compared with the WHO recommended rate of 12%).[94]

Women's experiences of powerlessness and lack of control in fertility management indicate a deep basic feminine morality that is somehow disturbed by modern contraceptive methods. When I was studying philosophy early in my undergraduate years I was impressed by a definition of morality as choice, based on the Latin derivation of the word. If morality is fundamentally about choice, then our deep feminine morality will be offended by experiences of powerlessness and lack of choice.

When women are dissatisfied with their contraceptive choices, what are they really saying?

I hear them saying that while the birth control methods offered by medical science may have offered some control of the rhythms and cycles of fertility, they have not offered a subjective, personal experience of empowerment or control. This makes sense in the light of the historical and anthropological material that shows how women's experience of fertility management has been affected for many generations by political and religious issues of power and control. The takeover of women's mysteries by patriarchal religions, scientific principles and technological solutions has demoralised us.

There is little doubt that there is still discomfort and shame attached to the functions of fertility, despite liberation in other areas of a woman's life. We live in a time when we are relatively well educated and appear to be free to choose in many areas of our lives, but many women still report an experience of ignorance, powerlessness, and lack of choice around reproduction and birth control. Whether or not we are having children, when we choose to have them, and how many we have, are topics of intense debate and opinion. The current phenomenon of increasing numbers of childless women in their late thirties and early forties is raising questions about personal, family and cultural beliefs and expectations.

It is time for you to consider what sort of birth control experience would be pleasing to your senses and your mindbody system. What would restore power, choice and control to your experience of contraception and the whole reproductive experience?

The invitation now is for you to consider new possibilities and decide which of the constructs in your current view of the world support you and which interfere with your ability to choose other ways of seeing and acting.

What other ways of knowing can support a practice like mindbody birth control?

Now that you have considered the information from mythology, history, and other cultures, what do you think?

Anthropology shows us that all people are educated and conditioned to adopt the values, beliefs and practices of their culture. People become bound by and to whatever belief systems contribute to the cultural consensus, limiting reality to a particular time and space[95]. So strong is the prevailing belief system in any culture that those who do something that differs from current consensus reality are described as being *resistant to enculturation.*

Resistance to enculturation is a term borrowed from Abraham Maslow, a psychologist who studied the human personality.[96]

Maslow is most well known for his investigation of the characteristics of self-actualisation, the optimal functioning of the healthy personality. In relation to the practice of mindbody birth control, there are two characteristics of self-actualisation that are of interest: autonomy and resistance to enculturation.

Autonomy is described as a relative independence from the physical and social environment, with a reliance on one's own latent resources.

Resistance to enculturation involves a particular detachment from the culture in which a person lives[97], and suggests adherence to one's own rules rather than the rules of society.

Maslow's work identifies some basic characteristics of autonomy in reproduction and in life. Like the Wayward Princess, women who develop autonomy and resistance to enculturation are responding and behaving in a way that differs from the prevailing cultural perception of reality. They are seeing with other eyes and hearing with other ears.

Part III

Matter and Psyche

CHAPTER TEN

THE ARCHETYPAL FEMININE

"Psyche" is a word from the ancient Greek meaning "butterfly". When we look inside, we begin a process of transformation that is like the caterpillar entering the chrysalis to begin the shift into a new way of being. I'm not sure exactly how the caterpillar experiences the transmutation in the cocoon, but I do know that our own inner experience of change and development can be just as remarkable.

Psyche was also the name of a young women in one of the ancient Greek myths. The story of Psyche and Eros tells of a woman's journey from unconscious absorption to a more conscious, differentiated awareness. Psyche began her life as a princess who was loved by all for her beauty, grace and charm. This adoration earned her the jealous regard of Aphrodite,

Goddess of Love and Beauty. As the alchemical Goddess of transformation, Aphrodite brought disruption and change into Psyche's life. Aphrodite sent her son, Eros, to make sure that Psyche was carried away by a demon. Instead, Eros, the God of Love, fell in love with Psyche and carried her away to his palace. Here they lived together happily, and everything Psyche wanted would appear as if by magic. In this way she was unconsciously absorbed in her day to day life. This is the romantic dream that captures many girls.

Why is this a problem?

Because it keeps women young and living an illusory life.

For Psyche, the missing element was that Eros would only appear under the cover of darkness and, therefore, remained unrevealed to her in a differentiated way. How often do we hear women complaining of their partner's unwillingness to really meet them in the way they want?

After some time Psyche became restless and began questioning her life, and she thus began the journey of developing consciousness. Her questioning led her to look upon her husband by the light of a lamp as he lay sleeping. He was burned by the oil from the lamp and fled from the revealing light. They were separated, and Psyche wandered, alone, encountering life's tasks and developing conscious relationship with herself and the world. Along the way she encountered Aphrodite as one face of the great mother Goddess. Aphrodite set Psyche four impossible tasks that involved sorting and gathering. With the help of various instinctual and spiritual energies, Psyche learned to sort and gather in a differentiated way. She managed to complete the tasks and so was reunited with her beloved Eros.

Eros in the myth represents Psyche's husband, but he also stands for the Beloved of the soul, that which connects us to our deepest sense of self. When we project all of our dissatisfactions and unfulfilled yearnings onto our partner or other people in our lives, we are not engaging the developmental tasks required for conscious relationship with ourselves and the world.

When a woman is waiting for someone or something to do it for her (as Psyche was when she lived in the palace), she is unable to assume the responsibility and maturity to make autonomous life choices. She is unable to fully engage her creativity and Eros for life.

Sorting the beans

When Psyche encounters Aphrodite, the Goddess sets four tasks that Psyche must complete before she can be reunited with Eros. We, too, have tasks we must engage before we can find our way to an authentic experience of ourselves and of the Goddess.

The first of Psyche's tasks was to sort a huge pile of beans and seeds presented to her by Aphrodite. As the alchemical goddess of transformation and one aspect of the mother Goddess, Aphrodite demands that we attend to her. This may be through the entanglements of a love affair or through an obsession with body image or through a

yearning for something unattainable. However She enters our lives, we can begin by sorting.

When a client first enters therapy, she often begins by pouring out all the beans and seeds of her life onto the therapy room floor. Together we then begin the task of sorting the huge pile of beans and seeds presented by life. Claiming autonomy also involves sorting the huge pile of beans and seeds given to us by the culture and our own personal inheritance and education.

Following Jean Houston[98], I have literally presented people with a jar of mixed beans to sort. You can fill your own jar at the supermarket or health food shop with as many varieties of beans as there are and literally pour out the beans for sorting.

In the myth, Psyche was not able to sort the beans and seeds with her rational, mental consciousness and was in despair about getting the task done. How many times have we all felt like that, when what is being asked by life seems too much for us?

Most women respond to the idea of mindbody birth control with "I could never do that" or "I couldn't trust myself to do that". What do those statements mean? Where does this lack of trust in managing our own mindbody systems come from? How can we sort out what is at work?

For Psyche, something had to arise from within the earth (from within matter, the body) to assist her. She was helped in her task by a multitude of ants who came to sort the beans. We are helped in this way by attending to the instinctual stirrings and intuitive wisdom that often first appears as irritability or an internal discomfort that can be like ants crawling over our skin, tiny inklings of what is calling for attention.

It is by attending to these inklings and sorting from within rather than by conditioned responses that we access the wisdom of the mindbody system.

For you, help may come in the form of dreams (day dreams or night dreams) as you are reading this book, in the form of body sensations and intuitive knowings. Several women who have read this material prior to publication reported strong reactions in the form of dream images, synchronistic life experiences, memories, and emotional responses.

The invitation is for you to engage a sorting process in relation to your own inner world, your body sensings, emotions, beliefs, facts, superstitions, and practices. Many of the sacred tasks throughout the book are actually ways for you to sort.

You can also literally pour out a jar of mixed beans and sort them. This is an opportunity for your inner wisdom to surface.

This sort of exploration belongs to depth psychology, an approach that respects the internal processes of psyche, both conscious and unconscious. Depth and mystery invite us to seek the meaning and value in our experience, to go beyond the appearance of things to what lies below.

Like many women, I was just doing it anyway, practising mindbody birth control without having to explain what I was doing. Once I decided to share the experience with others, I became interested in where the idea had come from, how I knew what to do, and what it meant to be doing it. Many of the answers came from Jungian psychology and the work that has developed from this approach.

Jungian or analytical psychology, based on the work of C.G. Jung[99], is in the tradition of depth psychology. In particular, it has described the feminine principle[100] as the archetypal energy that underlies fertility and reproduction.

Here we meet the Goddess as a psychological reality, in dreams and active imagination, and in the various symptoms and disturbances which call us to inner work. Like the ancient people for whom the Goddess was not just a philosophical idea, Jung discovered the objective reality of the inner depths of our psyches through his study of symbols and rituals throughout history.[101] In mythology across cultures, since the beginning of time, the commonality of images and practices is evidence that what we experience in our inner depths is real, as real as our waking reality. The images and symbols of the Goddess from our ancient past and from our dream life are part of the collective unconscious and carry meaning and value for our lives today.

Jungian psychology tells us that our personal experiences, both conscious and unconscious, rest upon an archetypal foundation in the collective unconscious. We all know that biological patterns of behaviour give us specific qualities, like the sucking reflex of a new born baby. Archetypes are the psychological part of these instinctual patterns, underlying our experience as fundamental templates of human experience.[102] What this means is that the archetypal elements of our experience are just as real as the physical, biological parts. Just as language and movement emerge from the mindbody system, so do tendencies like tenderness or aggression. Is it really only biology that prompts the child to take up a weapon and get to know his or her aggression? Or to nurture the cat or tend other children's war wounds?

It is as if Mars, God of war and Demeter, the mother Goddess, are entering those young lives to teach them about the mythical levels of experience. Of course, this is not always gender specific, but, like many modern women, I have been forced to acknowledge that boys and girls often do seem different .

While it is obvious that our lives are partly biologically determined, we also know that there are aspects of our experience that we can trace back through generations in our families. There are characteristics that make most sense when described through mythology or astrology, both of which recognise the archetypal or patterning energies at work in our lives.

When we accept that we are made up of both biological and archetypal elements, and that these are actually two poles of an interconnected reality, we open a door to a different sort of experience. This experience allows us to make sense of our dreams, our lives and our body symptoms in a different way.

James Hillman[103] and others have suggested that we ask what God or Goddess is calling for our attention in our disturbances, physical, mental, emotional and spiritual.

There is no definite, tangible way of describing an archetype. There is, in fact, an ongoing debate about what exactly archetypes are and where in the psyche they are located. While some approaches to this are more purely spiritual, Jung locates archetypes both within the body as well as psychically--in matter as well as in psyche. In this way, Jung's work approaches the idea of mindbody rather than splitting mind and body.[104] He was quite clear that we can only fully experience archetypes in embodied existence. Matter and psyche, mind and body, are not separate.

Many people think that archetypes are nothing but accumulated collective impressions. Jung did say that the images and symbols with which an archetype is represented do reflect this collective accumulation, but he was also very clear that an archetypal energy also has an existence all of its own.

I agree with Jung that archetypes exist in their own right as autonomous energies, although how we experience them will be determined by the time and place in which we live and our personal impressions. This directly affects the current experience of the Goddess as a force that is entering people's lives through dreams, story, art, and other forms.

If we consider the Goddess as *just* a symbol, albeit a powerful one, then we perpetuate a disenfranchisement that has been happening for thousands of years. If we recognise the Goddess as a manifestation of an autonomous presence that is calling for attention as we enter this new era, we are closer to an experience of the sacred in our lives. In other words, the Goddess is real and needs to be experienced in our bodies, our emotions, our day to day lives, not as a figment of our imagination but as a living presence.

The debate about where archetypal energy is located is also important to making sense of mindbody birth control. A *psycho-biological (mind-body)* process involves both *mind* and *body*, together; it is not about one acting on the other (as in "mind over matter"). It is a mutually interactive event.

The ancient philosophers, however, believed that mind needs to turn away from embodied experience to contemplate ideas, the pre-existing forms that are pure and eternal. This is central to Plato's debates[105], and, even if Descartes did not really intend a total separation of the thinking mind from the material world, his ideas have formed the basis of how we see the world today.

When Jung writes about the objective reality of the collective unconscious, he is not referring to this separation from embodied experience; he is emphasising the literal reality of the inner life[106]. For Jung, spirit and matter, archetype and instinct, are polarities of the one continuum of experience. The Goddess is not an abstraction or just a philosophical idea. As the Taoist adept, Zhou Xuaning, said,

> If you force empty sitting,
> Holding dead images in mind,
> The tiger runs, the dragon flies -
> How can the elixir be given?

The Goddess is not a dead image. She can become a living force in our lives if we welcome Her back.

The idea that behaviour and experience are guided and controlled by forces that are not personal has been described in many ways.[107]

Jung beautifully describes the archetype as

> an inherited mode of functioning, corresponding to the inborn way in which the chick emerges from the egg, the bird builds its nest, a certain kind of wasp stings the motor ganglion of the caterpillar, and eels find their way to the Bermudas.[108]

I am reminded of my grand-daughter's first visit to the bush when she was only a few weeks old. A flight of birds, disturbed by our passing, suddenly lifted into the air and the image of their forms outlined against the sky was reflected in her eyes. I could imagine this timeless image activating a pattern of response in her system.

There are forces within the psyche that profoundly affect our experience of ourselves and the world. By coming to know these, we know ourselves at a deeper level and have access to the accumulated wisdom of human experience. The archetypal feminine is a direct connection to the ancient mysteries of the Goddess.

There are now many books that describe how we can recognise an archetypal experience.[109] When we are gripped by strong positive or negative emotions, fascinations, compulsions, projections, and disturbing internal states such as anxiety or depression, there is probably an archetype at work. The one most of us recognise is "falling in love", especially the intense infatuation that seems to strike from nowhere. Of course, we know that Eros is shooting his arrows of desire, lighting up an aspect of ourselves we experience via the beloved. Or do we? It is sometimes easier to swallow the blue pill and go back to sleep, thinking that our emotions and fascinations are nothing but neurotic fantasies or unresolved problems from childhood. When Helen, Melanie and Donna were making their offerings to Aphrodite, Athena and the dark mother aspect of the Goddess, they discovered that behind their symptoms there was a Goddess calling for attention.

These women found images and symbols to represent the aspect of the Goddess they were engaging. These sort of images are specific to the archetypes yet unique for each person, so that archetype + experience = symbol. In this sense, every symbol is a mix of the personal and the collective, that which is individual and that which is universal. The image of Lilith is *my* experience of the archetypal feminine that came present through my dreams and active imagination. She may well look different for you. Archetypal images emerge from dreams, self-reflection and active imagination.

Jungian psychology tells us that dreams are transpersonal or archetypal expressions of patterns involved with life events.[110] My own dreams have informed my work, and I include some of them here as examples of how archetypal energies can come into our lives.

Once again, referring to the words of Jung,

> Together the patient and I address ourselves to the two
> million-year old man that is in all of us. In the last
> analysis, most of our difficulties come from losing
> contact with our instincts, with the age-old
> unforgotten wisdom stored up in us. And where do we
> make contact with this old man in us? In our
> dreams.[111]

For me it was an ancient woman who emerged in my dreams,
demanding my attention and leading me into an exploration of
the feminine archetype.

The archetypal feminine in dreams

During the time of researching and writing this book, the
theme of the archetypal feminine emerged consistently in my
dreams and in the accompanying journal entries and images. I
soon learned that this was not an isolated experience, but
something that was emerging synchronistically for many
people around the world. I was able to locate my experience as
one small part of the collective emergence of the "conscious
feminine", the new mythologem of the ancient Goddess "who
once ruled earth and heaven before the advent of patriarchy
and of the patriarchal religions".[112]

This theme first appeared in a dream (12.5.90),

> *My 14 year old daughter is pierced by pellets; 3*
> *marks on her chest which is young, pre-pubescent,*

flat. She has been shot. She is lying prone in a room with windows. Outside the windows a fire is burning, closer and closer. There is a sense of urgency. I am ringing for an ambulance, for help.

The female voice (European?) At the other end of the phone line is confused. And not responding quickly enough. My daughter is complaining of pain and my sense of the danger she is in is great. She cannot be moved.

The fire is moving closer and will burn us. A car outside ignites. The sense of urgency increases. Eventually the ambulance arrives. They say that she is not seriously hurt, that there are only marks on the surface of her skin. She is distressed, claiming deeper hurt. I am sure they do not understand the seriousness of the situation. My dilemma is whether to allow them to move her even though they do not understand the seriousness or whether to refuse to let them touch her. The fire burns closer.

At this time I was reading about the historical damage to women's ways of being. This damage is made very personal in the scene in which "my . . .daughter is pierced by pellets". The dream was asking me to find a personal response to the loss of feminine wisdom and mysteries during the transition from matrifocal to patriarchal culture. It was clear that this was *my* daughter who had been wounded, and I was being asked to decide who could be trusted to attend to this.

I have come to understand that each woman's personal response to the historical takeover of women's traditions is central to reproductive autonomy, and to the inner work to which many women are called in reclaiming ancient wisdom. What does it mean to *you* today that your grandmothers and their sisters not so many generations ago were persecuted, often just for being women? How does the deep wounding affect you personally?

Working with the dream, and allowing the dream to work with me, brought me closer to answering this question for myself. I wrote many journal entries like this one (4.6.90),

> *A theme of reconnecting with an inner, imperative demand which seems to contradict the rational external reality. It is as though the ancient Feminine has become lost within the rational Masculine approach to life; she can no longer be called upon to heal, leaving aspects of the Feminine bereft. Something new is called for.*

There was an inner, imperative demand to continue exploring the history of mindbody birth control. During this time I engaged an active exploration of the archetypal feminine, including regular fortnightly meetings with a small group of women to explore ancient traditional practices from the time of the Goddess. We based our rituals on information from the women's spirituality movement and the practices of witchcraft, paganism, Goddess worship, and celebration of the moon cycles in the style of the old religions.[113] These regular fortnightly meetings, coinciding with the full and dark moon cycles, continued for 12 years, providing a deeply appreciated ritual space for women's business. There is sanctuary, challenge and wisdom to be found in creating this sort of sacred container for honouring the feminine.

Women's Circle : Sacred Space for Women's Business

Consider forming a women's circle that works with the moon cycles. It is a meeting place that is not just social and that can support deep personal exploration. The actual content can take the form of chanting, singing, dancing, talking, meditating, guided inner journeys, drawing, painting, sculpting, enactment and various ritual processes. And, of course, feasting!

The group can be as large or as small as you are comfortable with. The traditional coven was made up of thirteen, but these days it is difficult enough to coordinate five or six women with busy lives. You can meet monthly with the full moon or fortnightly on the full and dark moon cycles.

I have worked in a women's circle in the Wicca tradition with the four elements of air, fire, water and earth and with the Goddess of many faces and names, in all her beauty, ugliness, strength, gentleness, wisdom, rage etc etc.

Working in a women's circle involves making a serious commitment to the regular meetings (monthly or fortnightly as suits the group) and deciding as a group how to proceed. There are a few basic ingredients:

• Having a ritual space that is safe and won't be interrupted. It usually works better to meet at the same place for most of the year, although some groups prefer to rotate through group members' houses.

• Deciding on a basic form for invoking the elements or quarters. I have used one like Starhawk's invocation in her book *The Spiral Dance*, where each of the elements is represented on an altar space and is called in to the circle at each meeting (and thanked at the conclusion of the meeting).

• Once the circle is cast, you can engage an activity that suits the group as a way of honouring the Goddess. Each meeting can be a group project planned beforehand by the whole group, or each person can take turns to offer the group an exercise. It is actually easier to take it in turns as it does not involve an extra meeting for the whole group to do the planning, and it is delightful to have the variety of experiences. This may seem difficult at first if you are not familiar with doing this, but it can also be done in pairs to give each other support.

If you have the time, it can be a rewarding experience to plan a ritual for each meeting as a whole group. In our circle, we did this for a whole year of full moons, working with the astrological sign of the full moon and taking time to decorate our ritual space and plan activities consistent with the moon sign and element.

Some of the less elaborate processes we have done over the years include:

- Washing each other's feet in steaming bowls of scented water as a way of honouring the feminine in each other with the element of water;

- Choosing a tarot card each and reading the description of the card so that each person can relate it to her life;

- Making something to represent a habit or relationship or whatever that we want to be rid of and performing a ritual burning or burial or sending out to sea;

- Selecting a particular experience (such as loss or desire or anger etc) and engaging a guided process of learning more about the experience and giving form to it by writing or drawing or movement etc.

- Reading poetry from ancient Egypt ...

Of course, each group is different and there are many possibilities for engaging in this way. The exercises in this book can be a guide.

The main requirements are a desire to journey with other women in sacred space and a willingness to take some risks and experiment in a safe context. The rest is up to you!

Reading for setting up a women's circle:

BG Walker, 1990, <u>Women's Rituals: A Source Book</u>, San Francisco, Harper & Row.

Starhawk, 1989, <u>The Spiral Dance: A Rebirth of the Ancient Religion of the Great Goddess</u>. San Francisco, Harper.

There are many books available on witchcraft, paganism and magic. These approach the work from different perspectives. Take some time to consider *your* sense of this work and develop your own rituals to honour the Goddess.

Once I had begun exploring this area, I had a number of dreams that deepened my relationship with my own internal feminine wisdom. I had been reading that

> the modern women's spirituality movement questions male claims to authority in the creation of ritual as well as in other theological matters. [114]

I realised that I had not questioned my internal relationship with male claims to authority deeply enough.

In one dream (6.5.92)

> *I am attending a workshop with people from all over the world. Part of the process is an excursion, like a school excursion. I am walking through a wooded area. The scene on the left is a painted backdrop, although it is so well painted that the closer I look, the*

more depth I can see, with trees visible a long way away. I am wanting to spend more time here just sitting. We are walking down to a gate where the male teachers are standing on an old cart pretending to whip everyone as they are walking through. It is a simulated scene from the Inquisition and they are saying, "Bow to Our Lady". I am saying, "I bow to the lady of the forest"" and they are whipping me. We are walking to a building where one of the teachers is baptising each person with warm water. I am standing back and after everyone is baptised, the teacher is asking me to come forward. I am saying, "No, I am not a Christian", and am walking past him. We are now forming discussion groups of four, and three of the others are hurrying over to discuss my response.

This same theme appeared several times over the next few years. One example is the dream (9.7.94), in which

I am living in a large house in a large country town. I am in church, sitting in the front with other women. We are talking with the priest who is lying on the floor. We are asking for an all women's day at the church. He is not wanting it but is not saying this directly. He is finally suggesting that the request will be put to the board for a decision. I am becoming more and more frustrated and angry with him. Finally, I am realising that he knows that the board will not approve it and that this is what he is wanting. I am angrily yelling at him. Some of the other women are very shocked.

I am now discussing this with the church board, a group of elders. They are not agreeing and I am arguing strongly and intensely. The other women are approving and supporting. Finally, I am yelling abuse at the group and one young woman is disapproving and saying that "No-one has respect for our elders any more".

I am at home and the children are playing. I am worrying about some sort of retaliation from the community for me abusing the priest and elders. I am checking the windows. Someone has already closed them and I am feeling protected. The children are playing inside and I am safe.

The idea of an all women's day at the church reminds me of the story my paternal grandmother told of meeting with the other women from her small Calabrian village, in the church on Christmas eve, to do women's business that excluded the men.

After seven years of exploring the archetypal feminine, I dreamed of a possible synthesis of masculine and feminine principles (26.7.97),

I am being shown around a huge cathedral by a priest. He is saying that he rents the space for Goddess workshops.

This idea of interconnectedness between masculine and feminine has been explored by Riane Eisler in her description of the partnership model of society in which,

> beginning with the most fundamental differences in our species, between male and female - diversity is not equated with either inferiority or superiority.[115]

She has strongly argued that our reconnection with the earlier spiritual tradition of Goddess worship and the partnership model of society is more than a reaffirmation of the dignity and worth of half of humanity. Nor is it only a far more comforting and reassuring way of imagining the powers that rule the universe. It also offers us a replacement for the myths and images that have for so long blatantly falsified the most elementary principles of human relations by valuing killing and exploiting more than giving birth and nurturing.[116]

My first image of the archetypal form of Lilith appeared in a dream and was terrifying (31.10.91),

> *a "demon" woman with hair flying . . . comes straight at my face . . . I am terrified and overwhelmed.*

Three months later (16.1.92):

> *Waking up screaming, heart thumping. Awareness of a woman's face coming up close to mine. Terror. No idea who she is or the context; just overwhelming terror.*

I experienced these dreams as "nightmares", dreams from which I woke terrified. I decided to draw the face that was flying at me in the night. This sort of attention to the dream image is consistent with Jung's idea that

> imaginatio is the active evocation of (inner) images secundum naturam, an authentic feat of thought or ideation, which does not spin aimless and groundless fantasies "into the blue" - does not, that is to say, just play with its objects, but tries to grasp the inner facts and portray them in images true to their nature.[117]

Drawing the image of the dream figure took me about twelve months. The feet were last to be drawn, and I recognised the characteristic owl's feet from an image I had seen once in a book. A search identified this figure as Lilith, a female figure dating from ancient Sumer[118] and from the Old Testament.

This was my first conscious knowledge of Lilith, and I became fascinated by the mythology and stories surrounding her. I have since learned that the image comes from the "Queen of the Night" relief, a Mesopotamian terracotta plaque held in the British museum. There is debate about whether the figure actually represents Lilith, Inanna/Ishtar, or Ereshkigal, Queen of the Underworld[119], but to me she is Lilith.

This image of the ancient feminine had came present from within my psyche, from focusing on my inner experience of the dream. In this way I was able to combine archetype and experience in a symbol that powerfully expressed my engagement with the archetypal feminine at this time. This image has continued to inform me over the years. When we are able to portray archetypal figures in a way that is true to their nature and ours, they continue working with us over time.

Working with the dream figure in this way also connected me to the living reality of psyche. One of the extraordinary and surprising aspects of this experience was the similarity of my image to the ancient image that many recognise as Lilith. She was the first woman, historically and mythologically, and was exiled to the darkness by a patriarchal religion that could not tolerate her wild feminine nature;

> The revolt of Lilith therefore expresses the rising up from below of all that would be denied by the rational, male consciousness.[120]

Somehow this ancient goddess had reached me asleep in my bed in 1991 and awakened my capacity to reconnect with long-forgotten mysteries. She has been reappearing in many women's lives through dreams and other inner work, prompting Jungian analyst, Betty De Shong Meador, to say that the "emergence of the archetypal feminine in her dark and light fullness" is an enormous transition equal to that which took place around 3500 BC:

> . . .the dissociation of the female element is a cultural phenomenon acquired through three thousand years of primacy of the patriarchal gods. In the archetypal pattern of the unconscious in our culture, the god An still trembles in terror in the face of the powerful, all-giving mother who holds men in the grip of the mother complex. The god Yahweh rages at disobedient woman and curses the dark reaches of the feminine, binding women to the demanding norms of the culture and to the negative animus.[121]

How could it be that the archaic feminine figure of Lilith had come to me in dreams and active imagination in the early 1990's, before some of this material was even available in Australia for me to read? The numinosity of her appearance left me in no doubt of the objective reality of her existence.

Yet, what does this mean, to experience a figure from my inner life as absolutely real?

Awakening one night in terror from one of Lilith's visits, I found long scratches along one of my arms. My rational mind wanted to explain the scratches as self-inflicted in the fearful scrambling to awaken from the terror, yet there was no sign on the other hand of the blood from the scratches, nor has this ever happened before or since in the tossing and turning that accompanies strong dreaming. I was reminded that Jung's primary knowledge of the archetypal figures of the anima in the form of Salome, and the wise old man in the form of Philemon, was derived from direct personal experience. His extensive research of these figures in the literature of myth, religion, and alchemy followed his own very real encounter with them.

When we consider the reemerging feminine, do we think of this as nothing but an idea that is coming back into inner awareness? Or can we recognise that this refers to a living, embodied experience that can be as real to us as our monthly bleeding, the frustrations and ecstasies of our lovemaking, the initiations of giving birth, and the transitions of aging?

I have certainly found this to be so, and for me this is closely linked to the ability to consciously regulate fertility through an internal process.

After drawing Lilith, I engaged a dialogue in active imagination with a feminine figure from a dream (26.3.92) who said,

> *I am tormented and often act angry and wild. There are energies in me which make me act in ways that others don't like, that make relationship difficult. I know that men find me hard to be with. I'm not like most women, I'm darker, wilder, more intense, more aggressive. Men don't like me. I probably should go*

and live on my own. The energy that moves in me is dark, wild, aggressive, not soft, motherly, agreeable, cooperative. I am that which flies at you in your dreams, screaming, scratching, wild, hair flying. I want you to love me. You take the attitude of the men who don't like me, you hold me off. I want to be seen, acknowledged, accepted, loved.

This statement was remarkably like the biblical descriptions of Lilith as the wild feminine who inhabited the nether regions as an outcast. She was asking to be seen, acknowledged, accepted, loved.

I met this wild feminine figure again in a dream three years later (30.4.95), in which *a dangerously mad woman is being kept under guard.* By this time, I had become very aware that our current culture is based on a history of brutal destruction and denial of mother-right. The dream was telling me that the rage and madness of the dispossessed feminine, personally and collectively, is poorly contained.

The feminine figures in my dreams and inner reflections were certainly insisting on an intensely personal engagement with the archetypal feminine material. This appeared yet again in a dream (20.11.92) in which

I am going to a house where I have things to do. My husband is ringing up to ask why I am taking so long. I am saying that both my grandmothers have asked me to do things for them.

If we interpret the motif of the grandmother in a dream as the manifestation of an archetype, as Jung[122] suggests, this dream can be understood transpersonally, relating to the collective unconscious. The archetypal feminine from both collective streams (mother and father lines) were asking me to do something for them. I heard them asking me to participate in recovering that which has been lost of the ancient women's mysteries, the fundamental task for women wanting to reconnect with the deep feminine wisdom of the Goddess. We will be frightened, shocked, overwhelmed, and repulsed by the screaming, scratching, wild woman who is clawing and calling her way back into our lives. Will we turn away and deny her again, or can we find the courage to see her, accept her, and love her?

Years later, I encounter the grandmother again (23.2.96), although this time she is much more powerful and sophisticated than I remember her. She has pretended to be an ignorant peasant woman but is really sophisticated and powerful, suggesting a development in my relationship with the archetypal feminine. The theme of reconnection with the grandmother continued (11.6.96),

> *I am eating vegetables which my grandmother has grown. I am nourished by these vegetables. I am wondering how it is that I am experiencing her so strongly now as she has been dead for over a year. I am also wondering how she could have grown these vegetables I am eating. I am wondering if she could have planted the seeds and someone else tended them and harvested them. I am also wondering about how*

the vegetables have come to me as my father would
not have been involved.

These sort of dreams bring with them the archetypal components of strong positive or negative emotions, fascination, compulsion, anxiety and other emphatic internal states. These are indicators that an unconscious, abstract process is becoming a living, embodied experience (that spirit and matter, mind and body, are meeting). These strong responses are also signs that there is sufficient energy in the mindbody system to make choices independently of current consensus reality. Unless we become actively and consciously affected by what is happening to us and around us, we cannot make conscious choices about our lives.

The capacity to choose in this way is important for mindbody birth control, as consensus reality would tell us that internal regulation of fertility is either not possible or is very risky.

The practice of mindbody birth control probably will not work for you if you just find the idea merely curious or interesting. Engagement and commitment will be needed, and some of the internal states you encounter may not be comfortable or familiar. Angela, whom I mentioned earlier, embarked on the practice of mindbody birth control with an optimism and a confidence in her ability to do this successfully. She encountered strong resistance from an inner masculine energy (via dreams and dialogue) who wanted to claim the territory as his own. Her journey with this was not comfortable as she had to confront her fears and doubts and her underlying dependence on the masculine in her life. She used many of the exercises from this book such as journal writing, focusing, drawing images, dialoguing with inner figures, and ritual processes. She courageously journeyed with the internal dynamics to find her way toward an empowered experience of autonomy.

CHAPTER ELEVEN

THE GODDESS IN ALL HER NAMES

Many years ago I lived in a rambling, old Victorian house that had settled so comfortably into the surrounding garden that ivy curled in through the vents and peeped up through the skirting boards. There was a large black house spider living in a web in the corner of the white wooden frame of my bedroom window. She lived there for years, expanding her web down the window until I carefully cleaned away all but the central part in which she nested. We were somewhat wary of each other and yet learned to live together in an uneasy accord. Her domain was the window corner, and if she should stray further afield, as she occasionally did in spring each year, I eyed her with suspicion and muttered incantations of protection under my breath. My domain was the rest of the room, and the times I strayed close to her corner to clean the window or replace a curtain hook, I imagined that she eyed me with suspicion and muttered arachnid warding off spells.

I knew she was female because she produced young, many tiny black dots to threaten my territory and expand hers. There was no sign of the male part in this fecundity, just the moving black flecks on the web. I usually relocated the babies by shifting their part of the web to a nearby tree or fence post when they seemed old enough to survive elsewhere, but certainly before they spread to overtake my bedroom. I can understand why she chose that particular corner. The window, looking out over bougainvillea and jasmine, caught the morning sun, there were no predators, and she apparently found sufficient food. Just as I never saw her mate, I never saw her hunt or eat. I suppose she did. One day I found a black spider's body on the carpet under the window. Momentary relief was followed by grief. I would miss her. Perhaps it was the elusive mate, because she was watching me serenely when I looked up.

Of course there is something absurd about having a relationship, albeit an uneasy one, with a black house spider. For what was I grieving for the few seconds I believed her gone? What is so attractive about the mix of repulsion and fascination I felt in her presence? It was a comfort to draw the curtain over her at night, yet I offered her a silent salute each morning.

I have come to understand my spider as a representation of the archetype of the archaic feminine, hidden from view yet ever so present. She lives in one corner of my psyche and is jealous of her possession of that corner. She will expand her territory if I am not watchful, and the balance is uneasy at times. She appears to control fertility regardless of the masculine; it is irrelevant to her despite what modern science tells us of reproduction. Sometimes I forget that she exists. Then I turn and catch a glimpse of her, and I always feel the shock of fear, excitement and recognition. She is eternal.

Most of us are ambivalent about coming to know this face of the archetypal feminine. Understandably so!

Present she is, yet so often unacknowledged and unwelcome. Although she now inhabits only a corner of our lives, the archaic feminine makes herself known via dreams, body symptoms, PMT, and moods. She is not always pretty or polite, and she has very little in common with contemporary cultural models of femininity. She is, in fact, remarkably like my black spider. So, I thank her for her presence, and for the opportunity to glimpse dimensions barely comprehensible to my rational mind.

She speaks to us whether we hear or not. She speaks through dreams, she speaks in images, she speaks in crystal clear imperatives that make no sense at all. And we ignore her at our peril.

We have moved so far in our fear of this ancient power that we use insecticides to rid us of spiders, and chemicals or gadgets to prevent conception. She would be more fully present in our lives if we would have her. And yet we are afraid, and perhaps rightly so. After all, we have been taught that the instinctual feminine is devouring and threatens to turn us to stone or absorb all back into unconsciousness if we are not careful.

We do not, however, need to kill her manifestations nor control her functions with such violence. She only appears so frightening and cruel to our civilised minds since we have forgotten how to worship and respect her life-giving role. In the form of the Hindu goddess, Kali, she has two faces: destruction and regeneration. We are so terrified of the destruction that we turn away before we glimpse her other face.

Once upon a time, a long time ago, a woman rested her hands on her belly and gave thanks to the Goddess for the new life stirring within. Her sister in the next village felt the blood begin to flow from her womb and gave thanks to the Goddess for preventing another pregnancy. For these women, the life-giving power rested solely with the feminine, a pact between women and the Goddess.

Once upon a time, women looked to the Goddess to bestow her blessings on conception and contraception. We know better now, for science has taught us that conception involves male seed at the right time in a woman's womb, and religion has taught us that women must honour the rational or spiritual logic of the masculine principle rather than the intrinsic rhythms of our own female bodyminds. We can control the process of conception scientifically, thus nullifying the age-old relationship with the life-giving power of the Goddess.

This sacred bond has undergone many changes over the centuries. Gone forever are certain mysteries of the old religion, women's mysteries of the cycles of sex, birth and death. Yet some of this lost wisdom is reappearing.

In the years since I began researching and writing this book, the shelves in my favourite bookshops, libraries, and online bookstores have become filled with works about the rediscovery of the Goddess religions, stories from mythology, and explorations of the feminine principle in myriad forms.

Like so many other women, I have participated in this changing consciousness through women's groups, ritual work, and creative expression through art and dance. Something is happening that is stirring people up, calling for attention. That something seems to be about human consciousness, about what it has been, what it is now, and what it might be in the future.

The collective emergence of the "conscious feminine"[123] is a phenomenon of increasing importance, reflected in the growing interest in the study of early matrilineal and matrifocal cultures, of the ancient religions which worshipped female deities (the Goddess in her many forms), and of mythology. There is an abundance of literature presenting views of the feminine principle from these perspectives[124], an area of study so widespread as to indicate a truly collective experience. It has been called a new mythologem, the myth of the ancient Goddess "who once ruled earth and heaven before the advent of the patriarchy and of the patriarchal religions", arising in response to the low point of a cultural development that has led us into the deadlock of scientific materialism, technological destructiveness, religious nihilism and spiritual impoverishment.[125]

What is the "feminine" to which so many are referring?

The feminine principle is understood to be present in men and women, although it is often through the functions of the womb that woman has connected to this through the rhythms and cycles of the earth and the elements. The earliest human attempts to record the passage of time are sticks marked with the lunar, or menstrual, cycle.[126]

A woman has a built-in cycle which connects her to this process of change, shedding the old to allow the growth of the new. It may be a little difficult to catch the rhythm of the cycle if it has been disrupted by contraceptive chemicals or stress, although it continues regardless. Conception, and therefore contraception, are traditionally the domains of the feminine. In many cultures it has been thought that for woman "to bear a child is the pact between her and the female Power of the earth"[127]. The consequences of invalidating the ancient pact with the feminine power of the Earth are far reaching.

We have broken this pact by claiming for ourselves the right to contracept with chemicals, disrupting natural cycles, "liberating" women from their fundamental rhythms. What of the rhythms that bind us to the Earth, and, therefore, together?

It is as if the feminine principle is returning to ask us to listen and attend to these rhythms, to remember the ancient pact. The problem is that this remembering does not come in a concise, ordered, logical form. It breaks through into consciousness as images, symbols, emotions of rage, fear, love, madness. If we hear voices, we are drugged or committed to institutions or are too afraid to admit it. If we see a message in the events or behaviour of those around us, there is treatment available for this also.

However it attempts to manifest, the message of the feminine archetype can all too easily be called some sort of pathology. There may even be a "cure" so that we remain "sane" (in agreement with consensus reality).

There has been a conspiracy to negate the influence of the feminine principle in the world. It began long ago, perhaps as men and women discovered the power to control Nature, and realised the potential for my will rather than thy will to be done. Christianity achieved a victory over Her influence in the world, turning "priestesses into handmaidens, queens into concubines and goddesses into muses".[128] The new religion of science and technology sealed Her fate; She cannot compete with chemical agents of life and death concocted in laboratories and sold for fortunes.

Yet it is naive to suggest a return to our original pact with the feminine power of the earth. We have woken, or been thrust, from the unconscious rhythms, woken to the power of rational thought and independent action. We have wrested some of the power of creation from the Gods and Goddesses. We have also taken the power of destruction for our own, and, if nothing else, it is this which awakens us to the necessity of remembering.

We cannot simply fall back into the ancient rhythms; more is required of us now. Even as Prometheus was bound for bringing fire to the mortals, so are we bound to the consequences of breaking the ancient pact with the Goddess. We can no longer sleep in Her embrace. We must awaken to the demands and chaos of the breakdown of the structures erected to replace the natural order.

Many women know that there is an inner rage that is buried in a layer of the unconscious often too deep to fully recognise or express. This breaks out in depression, eating disorders, and other "treatable" problems. It is important that we name these experiences for what they are: manifestations of a deep discontent with the disconnection from the natural rhythms of our feminine nature, of the Earth.

There is a long history of women being called "hysterical" (an emotional state named after the womb). Our emotions, moods, and intensity of expression have been labelled "irrational", and there are terrible stories of the psychiatric treatment of women who deviated from family and cultural expectations to find themselves. Jung began his work by taking schizophrenic women seriously, finding meaning in their images and stories. This deep respect for psyche supports us as we journey into unfamiliar territory in our emotions, our bodies, our dreaming and living. This journey teaches us that subjective experience can lead inwards to a world of uncharted territory, rich with sights, sounds and sensations, and that we have an inner life at least as vivid as the outer world. The dreams, images and words that emerge from within are our link to the deep feminine mysteries.

The Faces of the Feminine

When I talk about reclaiming feminine mysteries from ages past, what exactly do I mean by the "feminine"?

The feminine as a principle, a fundamental source, appears in a huge range of pictures and symbols arising across cultures since the earliest times of human existence. It is obvious that there are many different aspects of the archetypal feminine, many faces of the Goddess. In order to translate archetypal energies into personal experience, we need some interpretations of these many aspects.

An exploration of the Great Mother[129] archetype suggests two fundamental characters of the archetypal feminine: the elementary character and the transformative character. These can help us understand the forces at work in our experience of our own feminine natures.

Before we begin, however, it is important to remember that neither the Greek Goddesses nor these descriptions are meant to be definitive portraits of the nature of *woman*. They are different aspects of the feminine principle and, as such, can be, and are, developed by males when this is the cultural requirement, while masculine principles can be, and are, developed by females in a patriarchal culture such as our own. Therefore, the distinction between masculine and feminine principles is not determined by gender alone, but involves the historical background and culture in which a person lives. The work on the Great Mother is based on a study of collective symbolism, drawing from cross-cultural experiences of the feminine principle over time.[130] These are images and stories, rituals and practices that have informed people for millennia.

Elementary character of the feminine

The elementary character is that aspect of the feminine principle that is eternal, stable and life-giving and which resists change.[131] This is like Psyche's time of unconscious absorption in the palace with Eros. It is also like the conventional role of a doting mother who is totally identified with being a mother and immersed in the details of her day to day life and her children's well being.

While this may not be an attractive picture as a total experience, it is a very necessary function for nurturing, especially with small children. The difficulty many people have with this function is that we are childlike and dependent in relation to it. This is also the nature of the relationship between human and divine, and the basis of the ecological understanding that we are all the children of Gaia, the Earth, the Great Mother, and are dependent on Her to survive. It is not, however, a popular state in a culture like ours in modern Western countries, where we tend to value individual identity and strong ego development and personal achievement.

The elementary function involves a natural inertia that keeps us unconscious of many elements of our lives and pulls us away from maintaining consciousness. If this was all that was operating, Psyche would have stayed in the palace forever. We have all experienced the difficulty of holding certain understandings in conscious awareness; we can know something in one moment and then lose the connection in the next. The experience of waking from a dream only to have it slip away is a common example of this. It is this pull to unconsciousness that is at the basis of the elementary character of the feminine principle. In this state we tend to act instinctually, in automatic, unconscious accord with our impulses, moods and desires. This is the state of the young child whose responses are not mediated by conscious processing.

As consciousness develops, it forms an independent and relatively self-contained system that we experience as the ego or sense of self. As long as we can sustain the attention and focus required to maintain consciousness, we can be aware of what is happening in our inner and outer worlds. When we are conscious, there are links between our thoughts, images, memories, emotions, bodily sensations, and behaviours. When we can no longer maintain the attention and awareness required to be conscious, these links break down, and elements of our experience are pulled into the unconscious. This is what happens when we have made a determined decision to stop repeating a particular behaviour, only to find ourselves doing it before the day is out. Some of the links in the original conscious decision disappear, and the undesirable behaviour takes over in an automatic, unconscious sort of way.

This pull towards the unconscious can also be one element in the experience of depression. When the charge in the conscious system is reduced, our attention and energy is depressed, and the outer world ceases to hold meaning and interest. This may well be because something in the unconscious is calling for attention. I have come to understand that the experience of post natal depression is often linked to banishing the Goddess from our birth practices, leaving the new mother without the deep nurture and support of the archetypal feminine.

We are living at a time when the denigration of mothering has become destructive of women's ability to nurture. Women are no longer supported by previous generations of wise women, and modern birth practices with their emphasis on technology and intervention have brutalised women for so many generations in the "civilised" world that we have all but forgotten the tender care of sister midwives calling on the Goddess for a safe birthing. We now mostly give birth in hospital settings with medical intervention, and our babies are often taken from us to have their first taste of scientific technology before tasting the breast. Then we are told to break their hearts by letting them learn to cry themselves to sleep so that we don't make a rod for our own backs. And so it goes on, misinformation and denial of the instinctual wisdom of the feminine. No wonder so many women are depressed.

Depression may not, however, always be a completely negative experience. It may be the Goddess who is calling, depressing us, slowing us down so that we have some chance to hear her voice amidst the clamour of modern life. Sometimes we have to be pulled deep inside to even hear Her voice. As a culture, we have become so frightened of this call that we rush to relieve the depression with drugs or some other treatment that conspires to dull the voice of the Goddess.

Bestowing blessings

New mothers need the experience of the elementary function of the feminine. In one of the rituals which I offer new mothers, I sit behind the mother who is also holding her baby. We make sure we are all comfortable and are sitting with our bodies as close together as possible, sitting or lying down in a spoon position, back close against front. As we are sitting like this I match my breathing to the new mother's rhythm and talk about the lineage of mothers and say that just as her baby can feel her body and she can feel mine, the Great Mother sits behind all of us, holding us and supporting us in our nurturing. We sit like this for some time, holding and being held in the deep feminine mystery.

The transmission of this function has been lost along with so much of women's wisdom. It can be reclaimed. The antidote to the disconnection that leads to depression and other symptoms comes from women supporting women through our life transitions, trusting that the difficult experiences are not necessarily pathological but may be opening the way for a deeper connection to the feminine principle.

I find it disturbing to see reports of a decrease in the number of women who want to become mothers. It is as if the elementary character of the feminine principle is out of fashion. This disregard makes sense when we consider the emphasis on independence and individuality in contemporary culture (and it also makes sense in an overpopulated World). The elementary character does, however, have survival value for the species, from the individual mother nurturing her baby to the sustainability of the human relationship with the environment; it is more about "we" than "I".

Remember that the elementary function of the feminine principle is not a description of woman; it is a description of a function present in both men and women, representative of an underlying principle.

It can, however, seem that the elementary character of the feminine is somehow diminishing to women by linking us to the unconscious in this way. There is another way of seeing this. Many women are finding that the profound connection of the feminine to the unconscious can be the very substance of their lives. Through meditation, movement, creative expression, therapy, and other modalities, women all over the world are reconnecting with an inner world rich with meaning and nourishment.

Transformative character of the feminine
The transformative character of the feminine is the expression of a dynamic element of the psyche that drives towards motion, change, and transformation. This is like Psyche's journey to conscious differentiated awareness through engaging the tasks that bring challenge, development and transformation.

The process of life intrinsically involves transformation, yet the elementary character would turn everything back into its own eternal sameness. As the personality grows and is differentiated, we experience the transformative character independently, driving towards development, bringing movement and unrest. The transformative function of the feminine changes energy into life, gestates and produces new forms. One of the chants that has emerged from reclaiming the way of the Goddess tells us that *Everything She touches changes; She changes everything She touches.*

Many women experience the transformative character naturally and unreflectively in menstruation, pregnancy, and childbearing, in the dynamic interplay of relationship, and in ageing. When, however, a woman learns to reflect on her nature, she experiences the transformative character consciously, and she can fully participate in the experience of change and development. This distinction between the transformative character of the feminine as an unreflective function and as a conscious function has been important in my understanding of mindbody birth control.

When I began my mindbody birth control practice, I had emerged from a period of pregnancy, childbirth, and nurturing that was very much like the elementary character of the feminine. I then found myself in a period of unrest that was driving towards development and transformation. My capacity to engage this new phase reflectively has developed over time, from the initial self-enquiry necessary to develop the actual practice to the exploration of the wider implications of mindbody birth control presented in this book.

Obviously both aspects of the feminine principle are necessary. As with so many areas, the significance lies in the appropriateness of each function and the balance between the two. The transformative function is less of a problem in contemporary culture; we all like the idea of development and transformation. The challenge is to engage this consciously rather than adopting it as an ego ideal or a competitive process. Developing the capacity for reflection can help us to tell the difference.

The central question that Inanna asks in her descent to the Great Below is, "What is this?" (i.e. What is the meaning of this?)

While she journeys in the Underworld, Inanna is told, "Quiet, the ways of the Underworld are perfect and may not be questioned." When we are in the unconscious, we need to give up our rational mind questions and be guided by the "ants" and other instinctual stirrings.

When we return to the upper world, however, the questions about meaning and value become important. Knowing when to attend quietly and when to ask ourselves these questions as we move through life can help to restore the balance between conscious and unconscious, mind and body.

Self-reflection

There are many exercises that support self-reflection. Women are learning to keep journals in which they can writes hopes and fears, life experiences and learnings.

Women have always talked amongst themselves about the large and small details of their lives, a practice that has persisted despite the loss of the village well and the red

tent. It is likely, however, that the currency of these conversations is changing as women spend more time in the world of logos and become problem solvers in the rational mode. All too often, the talk moves quickly to "what to do" rather than staying with "what does this mean?" or "whom does it serve?"

One way to take the time to be immersed in an experience is to try an "inverted perspective"[4], so that instead of trying to fix something, you can take time to consider it from a different perspective. This process has been developed as a therapeutic strategy in the Gestalt tradition. To try this sort of focused reflection, follow these instructions:

Wherever you are, let your awareness wander, and notice something that stands out in your awareness, or something external that you return to and notice repeatedly . . . Now focus your awareness on whatever this is and become even more aware of it. What exactly is it like? . . . What shape is it? . . .What colour? . . . What does it do or not do? . . . Take some time to notice your impressions of it . . . Now change your experience so that you move into becoming this thing. Imagine that you are this thing (say to yourself, "I am the . . .")

Now, as this thing what are you like? . . . What are your qualities? . . . Describe yourself . . . "I am . . ." What do you do, and what is your existence like as this thing? . . . Notice what else you can discover about your experience of being this thing . . .

Now take some time to quietly absorb this experience. Rather than analysing your experience or thinking about it, write some notes or draw an image of your experience, or just notice how it is in your body sense and internal state.

For example, as I look up from my writing, I see a red shawl on the back of a chair. I notice its colour and the softness of the fabric. I enter into becoming the shawl, noticing the internal experience of this: "I am the red shawl . . .I am beautiful and I wish I was taken off the chair more often and out into the world where people can see me and enjoy my vibrant colour and intensity". A reminder to me to balance my introversion with extraverted colour and movement and to send this manuscript out into the world.

You may want to begin with a physical object like a chair or an ornament, moving to internal experiences as you become more familiar with the process. While this exercise begins with a somewhat artificial identification with the object (it seems obvious to rational consciousness that I am not a chair or a shawl or an ornament on the shelf), this sort of focused attention creates an opportunity for direct personal experience of new perspectives and understandings.

One example of this exercise involves paying attention to the experience of having a womb and then becoming the womb . . . "I am the womb . . ." What do you want as the womb? Are you willing to support mindbody birth

control? Is there something you want to say from this perspective?

Some women have found that even while their conscious intention is to prevent conception, when they become the womb in this way, there is an underlying desire for the womb to be filled with a baby. This is like Margaret Mead's idea of the relative "willingness and unwillingness to breed". Becoming the parts of us that may be willing or unwilling to engage change is one way to open negotiations with these internal parts so there can be an ongoing dialogue and negotiation between the willing and unwilling at the conscious level.

The goal of this exercise is the new information that becomes available through the perceptual shift; the identification with an inner part is the means rather than the end. There are exercises later in the chapter that work with disidentification to develop inner awareness (learning to attend to inner experience without being taken over by a response). There is a big difference between consciously identifying with something to explore meaning and value and unconsciously identifying with something that then determines how we respond.

When I began practising mindbody birth control, I spent time with this sort of identification exercise, exploring the bodily processes of reproduction until a solution emerged from the practice. It was as if I said to myself, "If I were the reproductive system, how would I prevent pregnancy; where in the process can it be interrupted?" The actual practice of internal regulation of conception emerged from within rather than from an external idea or instruction.

Deeper layers of meaning emerge from our experience when we consider it so closely that we are no longer on the outside of it looking in.

This experience of becoming something else can lead to an internal dialogue. Working consciously with self-dialogue encourages us to talk more to ourselves. Specifically, it involves asking, "What do I have to say to myself *about* this issue/experience/ desire/ etc.? What do I have to say directly *to* this? What does this have to say to me? How do I respond to this?"[132]

Talking to oneself about daily events or an important project is, of course, a familiar experience. It is possible to learn even more by engaging this deliberately and purposefully. Self-dialogue can take the form of internal conversations, journal writing, and dreaming. There are many famous discoveries which have emerged through a dream image.

Self-dialogue

One method used by many people I have seen in my therapy practice involves writing with both hands. The usual or dominant hand takes the role of the self and the other hand takes the role of the inner figure or other party in the dialogue.

An example of this is the dialogue between Mary and her belly about having a baby. Mary is thirty-three, has two daughters and has decided that she doesn't want any more children. She wants to develop mindbody birth control as

her main contraceptive practice but has doubts about whether it will work for her. While engaging a body focusing, she noticed strong sensations in the area of her belly and spent some time attending to these. She became her belly area by identifying with it and learned that it held an unwillingness to support her practice of mindbody birth control. She discovered that the belly had something to say, so she sat with a blank piece of paper and a felt-tipped pen and began the dialogue:

> Mary (dominant hand holding pen): *I want to talk with you about not having any more babies.*
>
> Belly (non-dominant hand holding pen): *Whose idea is that?*
>
> Mary: *Mine. Rose and Sarah are enough for me.*
>
> Belly: *That's only two.*
>
> Mary: *How many do you think I should have?*
>
> Belly: *Your mother had three, and her mother had three.*
>
> Mary: *I think two is enough for me.*
>
> Belly. *It's not up to you.*
>
> Mary: *Well, I want it to be up to me. What is it you want for me by having three children?*

Having identified the belly as an autonomous energy in her inner world, Mary was able to continue the dialogue in this way and also through drawing and enactment. She entered into a process of negotiation, and when she asked the belly what its interest was in her having another child, she discovered that the belly believed she would be wasting her life if she stopped at two children. When Mary explained that she was studying natural medicine and wanted to work to make people well, the belly softened its attitude but insisted that if Mary failed to commit herself to her work in the world she should have another child.

An important element in this sort of negotiation is to find out about the interests and beliefs of the internal part. If we just stay with the position of the part, we are stuck.

Mary's belly held a position that she should have three children because her mother and grandmother had. There was also a belief that this choice was not up to Mary. The belly was, however, motivated by an interest that Mary not waste her life. This was something that Mary and her belly could agree on !

Sometimes the negotiation can be this simple, with the part willing to consider an alternative. At other times, the negotiation can become more complicated as other beliefs are involved. The belief that the choice was not Mary's had its roots in the generational experiences of the women in Mary's mother line. The choice had not been theirs, and the ancestors, as internal patterns, did not want Mary to have this choice either. In this case, the internal "mothers" believed that it would be unsafe for Mary to claim reproductive autonomy. This can be traced to the sort of historical experiences explored in Part II.

This sort of internal dialogue with autonomous inner figures takes us back to the territory of the objective reality of psyche, the idea that what we find in our inner world is as real as the outside world. Jung called this "active imagination", a process that is different from fantasy and daydreaming because we recognise the *literal reality* of the experience.[133] In active imagination we respond as if the imaginal sequence were an actual waking situation, by having authentic responses and being genuinely affected by what is revealed. This sort of engagement develops our capacity for self-reflection.

You may find yourself talking to your womb, or to the inner figure responsible for conception or contraception, or to the Goddess or another deity. If the dialogue becomes spoken rather than written, you can support it by using an empty chair or a cushion or an object to represent the "other" with whom you are interacting. In this way you are supporting the reality of the experience and encouraging the rational mind to accept the objective existence of the other aspects of your experience.

Pillow talk

I have engaged the following process with women who are mourning the loss of a child through miscarriage, abortion or infertility, or when the choice to not conceive involves a sense of loss.

Place a small cushion in your arms and invite yourself to speak with the unborn child. This is always a deeply emotional experience and there can be a deep sense of communion with the child who has not or will not be born. Women have talked of hearing or sensing the child's

responses to the communication, and the experience is one of healing and forgiveness.

You can do this yourself as an ongoing practice by finding or making a pillow or rolled up piece of fabric that represents the baby. Some women make a sort of cloth doll with face and clothes while for others a more abstract bundle or cushion works. Commit to spending 10 minutes each day with the baby, noticing any thoughts, feelings or body sensations.

It is important to use this time as an opportunity to notice and experience your authentic response. There is nothing in particular that should or should not happen in this exercise. You may find yourself talking with the baby, sharing hopes and dreams or regrets and disappointments. You may experience strong feelings of sadness, anger, longing or other responses. Some days you may forget to do the exercise, but if you make a commitment to do this for one month (one whole cycle) even the days you miss will teach you something about your relationship with this area of your life.

Women have been surprised by the strength of connection with the baby, with both negative and positive feelings coming present. It is important not to censor your responses in this process. Women have been "making nice" for a long time, and feelings like rage and grief need permission and acceptance. This can be a powerful exercise, and you may need support with the responses that emerge. This may take the form of talking with someone close to you or seeking out a therapist or counsellor. It can

be important to have someone witness and validate your feelings and offer support.

While the transformative aspect of the feminine principle is always present in women, only some women experience it reflectively or consciously. This explains how some women are able to practise mindbody birth control, consciously regulating a biological process like conception.

In my experience, there was clearly a shift from relatively unconscious, automatic behaviour to a more reflective, consciously considered approach to fertility. Amy, the woman who spoke of tribal cultures, described her relatively unconscious experience of mindbody birth control:

> *I was probably not surprised about this, just a fairly natural understanding and acceptance coming from a fairly unconscious level.*

And Sandy, a natural health consultant with her own successful business, three children, and a new marriage,

> *When we (women) are really doing things we are just doing them, and then people ask us and we say, "Well, I just do it".*

When the transformative character of the feminine is experienced unreflectively by women in menstruation, pregnancy, and childbearing, we are just doing it. Amy and Sandy both experience mindbody birth control unreflectively, just accepting it as fairly natural, a process they are just doing.

I have already mentioned the many women who do not claim to practice conscious control of conception, yet describe so called lucky experiences of not conceiving over extended time periods. Jenny, settled now with three children, talks about her time travelling in her twenties:

> *I was quite sexually active with a number of sexual partners and never in that time practised any form of contraception. The only awareness was that I did not want children, but there was no practice or awareness. I did not conceive.*

She was just doing it anyway!

Most of the women consciously practising mindbody birth control described a relatively stable period of at least two consecutive pregnancies and births prior to their decision to not have any more children; a period of time that is like the description of the elementary function as conservative, stable and unchanging. Three of the women described their experiences of repeated pregnancy and childbirth, in retrospect, as a predominantly unconscious drive to reproduce, to meet previously unmet nurturing and other needs.

One woman linked her desire to become pregnant with *emotions mainly of vulnerability and wanting nurturing.*

For another it was about coming to *know the very needy little girl who just wants to be held, not have sex.*

For another, successfully practising mindbody birth control involved working through the issues around letting go of her youngest child when he turned seven, a time when she could possibly have become pregnant to *fill the gap*.

These responses all demonstrate a capacity to reflect on internal processes, thereby supporting change and development. When we make the time to notice what we are experiencing and have some ways to process our experience, we become more able to make conscious choices about our lives.

Attending to dreams

Another way to find your own experience of the feminine principle is through your dreams. If you are not already doing so, have a journal by the side of your bed to record your dreams, either during the night or when you wake in the morning. Just a word or a feeling sense is enough to start with or when you are busy.

As you are able to record dreams consistently, you can begin to collect the feminine figures from your dreams, drawing them and placing the pictures where you can see them, and they can see you. You can begin dialoguing with the dream figures, either by talking out loud (if you're not too self conscious) and listening quietly for the responses with your inner ear, or by writing a letter with your dominant hand to the dream figure and then letting the dream figure respond with your non-dominant hand.

The practice of writing a letter that is not actually going to be sent is also a powerful exercise in expressing unthinkable thoughts or unspeakable things. Writing without censoring to inner and outer figures can allow a freedom of expression that clears the way for new connections and understandings. That sort of letter can then be burnt or buried in the garden.

CHAPTER TWELVE

THE MASCULINE PRINCIPLE

Just as the elements of the feminine principle emerge from archetypal reality, so do the elements of the masculine principle. We can see this in the patriarchal myths that still underlie the modern world view. These myths have, however, become unconsciously accepted as absolute truth, determining beliefs, social values, and the current religious attitude to science. [134]

The basic character of the archetypal masculine has been described as rationalising, abstracting, and controlling, as in the myths of one supreme male God: the Judeo-Christian Jehovah, Allah in the Islamic world, and Zeus in ancient Greece, a king-like energy also personified in ancient and modern heroes. Psychologically, the masculine principle represents an emphasis on individual focus, rational intentionality and personal will; a sense of personal identity that rests in a separate self answerable to the law of the Father as God or King. The archetypal masculine has been described as focused, divisive, and assertive, in contrast to the archetypal feminine that has been described as diffuse, connective, and receptive. Obviously both men and women can embody these qualities. Understanding and experiencing the differences can allow us to develop choice about which principle we call on in our lives.

Patriarchal consciousness is in the territory of eternal spirit, that which always was and always will be, a position fundamentally opposed to the genetic principle, the principle of creativity and generativity that underlies aspects of feminine consciousness.[135] This reflects the philosophical stance of Socrates, Plato and Descartes in which all that is pure and constant is incorporeal, not of the body, with little place for subjective embodied experience. I have often wondered if the strong attraction to Eastern spirituality arises in part from this philosophical idea of eternal spirit. It is as if two generations of disillusioned Westerners have turned to Buddhism or Hinduism without fully realising that they are still caught within a transcendent philosophy that denies the creative principle of feminine consciousness.

It is, however, a confusing task to sort this particular pile of beans and seeds. There is a fundamental paradox in patriarchal consciousness, as it cannot avoid the use of nature symbols except in abstract conceptualisations such as mathematics.[136] As symbols of the feminine principle, however, the life-giving nature symbols do not belong in patriarchal consciousness. Even while it attempts to distort and degrade the nature symbols, patriarchal consciousness wants to take over the creativity of the life-giving power of the feminine. This can be seen in ordinary English language. The following sentences show words relating to the life-giving aspect of the feminine being applied to activities or projects of 'masculine" creation;

> Our nation was <u>born</u> out of a desire for freedom.
> His writings are products of his <u>fertile</u> imagination.
> His experiments <u>spawned</u> a host of new theories.
> Your actions will only *breed* violence.
> He <u>hatched</u> a clever scheme.
> He *conceived* a brilliant theory of molecular motion.
> Universities are <u>incubators</u> for new ideas.
> The theory of relativity first <u>saw the light of day</u> in 1905.
> The University of Chicago was the <u>birthplace</u> of the nuclear bomb.[137]

A more recent addition might be: I <u>create</u> my own reality!

It does seem that the root metaphor for creativity in the English speaking world is procreation, a predominantly feminine function. What patriarchal consciousness does, however, is translate the feminine function of creativity into activities and projects characterised by masculine principles, leaving the feminine principle without the pride of creation. And leaving many of us confused about the philosophies and spiritual paths we adopt.

The archetypal masculine in dreams

 In some of my dreams, the masculine figures have resonated with the description of the god Yahweh who "rages at disobedient woman". This theme appeared in the form of a priest who first appeared (20.11.90) wearing a cowl, with its association as a monk's hooded garment.

> *I am visiting a house in the mountains. The house is run down but habitable. The forest and mountains are beautiful. As I am walking up the mountain with my three daughters, I see a cowled figure at the top of the hill. He appears faceless. We sense evil and go back down to the house. The house belongs to a male friend who lives here with his mother and wife. He asks what we are sensing and when I tell him he says, "No wonder my mother's so crazy, we've lived here many years". I am digging in the ground. I am told by an inner voice to stop excavating. I realise that the surrounding mountains are so high that there is no need to keep digging as all we have to do is make a lip in the top of the ridge and whatever is there will run over the edge to us. I am concerned about the evil of the hooded man but am assured by an inner voice that if it comes in small amounts it will be safe.*

The cowled figure was a force sensed as evil, and which was responsible for making the mother crazy. The suggestion in the dream was that the evil could be managed if it comes in small amounts. I understood the dream to be saying that the evil that has made the mother crazy is the collective damage that has been done to feminine, instinctual ways of knowing. I was aware that not so long ago, perhaps 400 years ago in certain parts of the world, a woman doing what I was doing, both in terms of the birth control practice and writing about it, would probably have been accused of witchcraft and may well have been tortured and killed. "No wonder my mother's so crazy!"

It is difficult to grasp the implications of the mass extermination of talented, unconventional, or simply unpopular men and women during the Inquisition, an event that has profound personal implications for creativity and autonomous expression to this very day.

The priest figure reappeared in the dream (6.5.92) mentioned previously in which a male teacher figure was whipping me for refusing to bow to Our Lady. While the first priest figure was faceless with an impersonal quality, this teacher figure was more differentiated and personally related, although still belonging to the collective setting of a school. The next appearance of the priest was in the dream (9.7.94) in which I was asking for woman's day at the church; this priest was opposing my demands, and I was fearful of the consequences of antagonising him, although I found a safe haven at home.

The strongest association with these dreams is to the historical information about the religious and political takeover of women's ways of worship and healing. They reminded me again and again to find the personal meaning of the historical and political information. The true horror of the Inquisition and the implications for the practice of women's mysteries were becoming clearer to me during the time of these dreams. I was immersed in reading the literature relating to this and also reflecting on the meaning for women now. What did all of this information mean to me as a woman living in Australia and in the 1990's? What does it mean to you today?

It is easy to relegate events like the Inquisition to history. The process of reflection and incubation has, however, led me to understand that the God who rages at disobedient woman is not just an historical artifact or something taken in from an authoritarian personal father; it is a collective phenomenon that still profoundly affects the way women and men live their lives.

Mindbody birth control is a simple practice, but very few women spontaneously develop it, and most women doubt that they can successfully use it. This is one example of the profound and lasting damage done to the creativity and autonomy of women over the last few thousand years. The destruction of women's wisdom and mysteries means that it takes strenuous effort and much courage for a woman today to find her way to the inner ground of true feminine wisdom and strength. For many women, it will be easier to disbelieve or ignore the possibility of mindbody birth control (and other creative life choices) than to confront the legacy of terrible, aching loss and terror in their deepest selves

The discontinuity of oral traditions during the time of the Inquisition has profound implications for the practice of reproductive autonomy, personal autonomy, and the engagement of women's mysteries. I also felt a very personal implication as my research developed.: a response of fear about revealing this material. This was reminiscent of my dream in which a fire is burning closer to my wounded daughter (the Inquisition has also been called the "Burning Days").

Even though I knew rationally that there was no current tangible threat of persecution for exploring this material, there was still a fear of attack for exploring a practice that had, in all probability, been the cause of persecution at other times in history. To propose a method of birth control that offers women true reproductive autonomy is radical, and some of the accompanying ideas are subversive in relation to current consensus reality. However, it is clearly not a dangerous undertaking these days! There may be people who will object spiritually, morally or politically to some of the material explored in this book, but my fearful response was irrational and out of place in the current times. It did, however, raise some important questions about the impact of cultural-historical conditioning.

I have observed that anxiety often accompanies an exploration that deviates markedly from current consensus reality. The drastic and usually fatal treatment of anyone who deviated from the collective rules at various times and places throughout human history has left a legacy of a sort of collective paranoia that is alleviated by conforming to consensus reality. It is easier to stay quiet, conform to the rules, and not take risks. It is easier to stay with our illusions, even when we are dissatisfied and depressed. This is consistent with Maslow's observation that qualities such as autonomy and resistance to enculturation are not easily developed. So much has been lost.

The theme of masculine takeover of feminine ground also appeared in a dream (23.4.98), in which the masculine figure was not a priest but appeared in the more personal form of father, although the practice of calling priests "father" in the Catholic church is suggestive of this link. In this dream,

> *I have been travelling for a long time and having many adventures in remote places. I am now at home in my parent's house. I am wanting to sleep. My father is intruding into the room and claiming that everything in it is his. I am leaving.*

This dream occurred in the final year of writing up the thesis and presented a familiar theme of masculine dominance. In reflecting on this dream, I was reminded that the Greek myths presented the stories from the perspective of the fathers, so that the Goddesses were defined in relation to the masculine, rather than in their own right. In ancient Sumer, Inanna, descending in her own right to meet the queen of the Underworld, was a very different figure from Persephone who was abducted by Hades, the masculine ruler of the Underworld in ancient Greece. I now see that the archaic feminine figures that had been emerging in my dreams and active imagination were making this point all along!

It seems that I may have finally received the message by the time of the dream in my father's house since I do leave the situation. This is repeated in a dream (11.11.98) in which "*I am leaving my parent's house as something has happened which I am not happy with*".

Jungian analyst, Marion Woodman wrote a book called *Leaving my father's house: A journey to conscious femininity,* in which she described the experience of relating to the emerging feminine,

The eternal feminine is thrusting her way into contemporary consciousness. Shekinah, Kwan Yin, Sophia, whatever her name, she is the manifestation of the divine in matter . . .Knowing her has nothing to do with blindly stumbling toward a fate we think we cannot avoid. It has everything to do with developing consciousness until it is strong enough to hold tension as a creative energy . . .It is our immediate task to relate to the emerging feminine whether she comes to us in dreams, in the loss of those we love, in body disease, or in ecological distress. Each of us in our own way is being brought face to face with Her challenge.[138]

Our personal work with dreams, active imagination, focusing, and reflection is an essential part of being brought face to face with Her challenge. For me, the tension has, at least in part, been between the masculine and feminine principles in my own psyche. This tension is also present in the collective psyche, demanding a new resolution as we approach a new era.

So many women find themselves engaging Her challenge and then discovering the internal forces arrayed against developing relationship with the ancient feminine wisdom in the psyche. It may be a critical "father" figure demanding obedience to the laws of rationality and reason. It may be a dark, terrible "mother" figure, destructive in her envious, bitter rage. When we persist, we discover the Gods and Goddesses calling for attention, and we learn ways to engage these inner figures and form relationship with the masculine and feminine elements in the psyche.

A dream (4.8.98) that came during the final writing up of the doctoral thesis seemed to make the priest redundant,

> *Something is being made and there is much discussion about the details of the making. A voice is saying, "It's between you and the maker".*

If the priest is understood as the one who traditionally mediates between the divine and the personal, interpreting the relationship according to the particular laws of his calling, then a direct relationship with the 'maker" does away with the middle man and his constructed laws.

There were also dreams that showed me that this work was altering the internal dynamic with the archetypal masculine. Early in the development of the thesis I dreamt (29.10.91) that

> *I am working in a therapy session with two women. My Grandfather is in the room observing. As the work is moving into a very painful area for one of the women, I am continuing to confront the dynamics of the process by saying, 'so, it's to and fro, up and down, back and forth.." She is sobbing. My grandfather is groaning and clutching his heart. We are carrying him out of the room. His skin is very grey. The rest of the family, Grandmother, mother, and sister, are gathering round and an ambulance is called. I am thinking that this is definitely not my fault, not my responsibility; he did not have to be in there if he did not want to. Now my father is sitting in a chair holding his chest. He has been having signs that he is about to have a heart attack. The pain is*

intensifying and he is saying," If this keeps up it will end with me dead". I am thinking that it may not need to, but he seems resigned.

The motif of the "grandfather" can be understood in a similar way to the "grandmother"" as an archetypal element. The work I was doing was threatening the masculine elements in my psyche;

If this keeps up it will end with me dead.

A dream (6.9.92) one year later also reflected this theme as, in the dream, I put down the responsibility for keeping a crippled masculine figure alive,

I am wired up to a man in a wheelchair so that the constant contact is helping with his healing. I am available for him like for a baby. I am constantly responsible for attending to this man's needs for attention and nurturing so he can get better. We are walking and I am pushing the wheelchair. I am generally admired for my altruism and devotion to healing by carrying these wounded men so they can recover. I am in a building that is under construction. I am putting down the man (or the wiring that connects us). He appears to be sleeping but I am wondering if he is dead and am aware of my responsibility to him. I am talking with others about something technical and I am the only one who is understanding what is being discussed.

This is a familiar image to many women who reach a time in their lives when something within signals that it is time for a change of orientation from the masculine principle to the feminine. Finding the strength to put down what we have been carrying for the masculine is the beginning of reclaiming the inner ground of autonomy and choice.

Who or what are you supporting in the masculine, in your inner world, in your work place, in personal relationship, in your family?

Like Angela, who deferred to her father and did not journey to the red waterfall in her dream, many women defer to an inner or outer masculine figure who appears powerful but is dependent on the woman's compliance. Freeing ourselves from this entangled relationship is essential to being able to live fully and creatively.

In my life, the context for transformation has been my experience of the archetypal feminine. This has demanded a change in the balance between the masculine and feminine principles in my psyche. The archaic, magical, and mythical feminine images and voices have formed the core of this process. It was the feminine figures in dreams and active imagination who insisted that I engage this task as a personal exploration, telling my soul story as one part of the new mythologem of the emergence of the archetypal feminine.

When Marion Woodman describes women's dreams, self-reflective writings, and images as "soul stories", she is also naming the synchronicity of the inner exploration arising for women in many parts of the world.[139]

My dreams, journal entries and reflections formed and directed my study of mindbody birth control. My experiences have convinced me that the archetypal feminine is a force that is alive and well even after thousands of years of banishment, a force that informs our exploration of women's mysteries and, at times, demands that we do so. My dreams also reflect a struggle with the balance of masculine and feminine principles that many women experience; I have seen this in clinical practice and have read about it in the ever increasing number of books written about the inner journey. The dramatic imagery in some of my dreams reminds me that this is serious business. There is no doubt that the loss of feminine ways of being threatens our existence as a species, from the basic principle of mother right to the respect for Nature and the reverence for life in general.

Reclaiming these feminine ways of being is more difficult than it would first appear. As we have seen, there are collective forces that would keep us from the embrace of the beautiful, powerful woman deep within, the Great Mother, the Goddess in her many forms.

As an example of this, many women are frightened to consider mindbody birth control. It is a simple practice that asks us to reconnect with our deep inner body wisdom and to trust the authenticity of the mindbody relationship. Yet it is also a practice that stirs up historical, cultural and spiritual issues that have their roots in the very essence of what it is to be a woman in the lineage of the Goddesses of the ancient world.

To be born a woman today means that you are a daughter in an unbroken line of mothers and daughters back to the beginning of time. To reclaim even a part of the wisdom of this heritage, to remember the true life-giving power of the feminine, challenges thousands of years of conditioning that wanted us to forget.

Dare you remember?

CHAPTER THIRTEEN

CREATION, PROCREATION, AND CREATIVITY

We have seen how the English language tends to confuse creation and procreation. The consequence of this is a robbing of the fundamental feminine experience of creativity. It has, for example, been argued by contemporary feminist writers that the activities of reproduction cannot represent conscious creativity.

For example, Simone de Beauvoir suggested that

> the woman who gave birth, therefore, did not know the pride of creation; she felt herself the plaything of obscure forces . . . But in any case giving birth and

suckling are not activities, they are natural functions; no project is involved . . .[140]

In her examination of the issue of creativity vs generativity, Erica Jong proposed that "creativity requires active, conscious will, while all pregnancy requires is the absence of ill-will toward the foetus."[141]

And once again, de Beauvoir,

> ensnared by nature, the pregnant woman is plant and animal, a stockpile of colloids, an incubator, an egg . . .Ordinarily life is but a condition of existence; in gestation it appears as creative; but that is a strange kind of creation which is accomplished in a contingent and passive manner.[142]

These statements are describing reproduction as an unconscious function of Nature, consistent with the elementary character of the feminine. In this description there is no room for conscious participation in, or control of, the process. It is ironic that writers such as de Beauvoir and Jong, whose work has served to empower women, seem, in fact, to have gone along with the culturally conditioned view of reproduction as ensnarement by Nature. They are saying that creativity requires an activity or project that is not simply a natural function but which involves conscious, active will, thus rendering procreation something other than creativity in their eyes.

The main theme of the feminist argument was: *Just because women are built for it, does not mean they have to do it, nor that it is the only thing they can do*. There is, of course, a truth in that. Yet in the struggle to free themselves from the biological necessity to reproduce, women seem to have ceded a final victory to the socio-cultural forces that denigrated the life-giving power of the feminine.

Many of the debates about motherhood, from the early feminist writings to current discussions of childlessness and the myth of having it all, reflect a disenfranchisement that occurred many thousands of years ago. In this context, de Beauvoir's statement about being the "plaything of obscure forces" becomes an expression of what we have lost.

One of the (perhaps inevitable) errors of the feminist mythology has been caring more for a politics of equality based on a masculine standard than for developing a true respect for an intrinsically feminine philosophy and experience.

In a psychological sense, the historical shift has been from one polarity (feminine principle) to the opposite (masculine principle), and the current collective re-emergence of the conscious feminine is yet another shift. Hopefully this current shift will correct these ideas about women's passivity in conception, gestation, birth and nurturing. The potential for action is fundamental to the feminine principle. There is creative choice in reproduction.

When we begin to claim back the pride of creation in pregnancy and nurturing, we begin to develop conscious awareness of a previously unconscious process, a critical threshold in developing our full potential. As we have seen, the transformative character of the feminine can operate either unreflectively or reflectively. As one aspect of this, procreation can, therefore, be experienced either consciously or unconsciously and automatically. Many women today are increasingly aware of participating consciously in pregnancy, birth and parenting. These are, however, still processes which can easily happen with little or no reflection or conscious awareness.

It may be that the process of conscious reflection is what is missing for women who, like Jong and de Beauvoir, experience procreation as devoid of the pride of creation. For them there is no reconciliation of the unconscious or instinctive desire of the elementary character of the feminine with the awakening consciousness and movement toward change of the transformative character of the feminine. This comes back to the basic mistrust of the elementary aspect of the feminine. This mistrust interferes with the development of true feminine consciousness, robbing women of wisdom and conscious choice in birth control and so many other areas of life.

How can we reconnect with the elementary feminine?

Through the body, through the embodied experience of being a woman.

One part of this is the instinctual drive to reproduce. These days, this instinct has become unfashionable, as if it is somehow insulting that women should be subjected to such a thing. There are now questions about whether such an instinct really exists or whether it is some sort of trick perpetrated on women to disempower them. It is vital to recognise the source of these ideas in patriarchal consciousness.

We do not have to deny the elementary feminine to exercise choice and empowerment. The confusion seems to be in attributing the loss of power and control to the elementary aspect of the feminine principle rather than to the cultural and religious forces that have robbed women of access to the deeper wisdom of the feminine. There is not something wrong with wanting to have babies or growing them in our bodies or suckling them at our breasts. The sense of wrongness comes from the historical takeover of women's life-giving powers. The current trend away from respect for mothering may be the final victory for the masculine principle.

The clear decision to change the pattern of repeated pregnancies and have no more children that is described by many of the women practising mindbody birth control is consistent with the transformative function of the feminine that drives towards motion, change, and development. The women with whom I spoke were more likely to explain their experiences in these terms than talking about rational intellect or personal will. Transformation is a fundamental aspect of the feminine principle.

When she studied reproduction from a cultural perspective, Emily Martin found a whole range of metaphors as symbols of birth. Across cultures these describe an inner process of significance and meaning that is connected across time.[143] When this is recognised, the pregnant and nurturant woman is seen as an initiate, undertaking a transformative rite of passage, rather than someone at the mercy of nature. Birth as a rite of passage is often celebrated in ancient birth songs, prayers and stories.[144]

The experience of conscious, internal regulation of conception is also a transformative process. When women consciously engage their reproductive choices and determine meaning and value in these for themselves, they are reclaiming true reproductive autonomy.

Creativity and transformative choices

One of the elements in women's experience of mindbody birth control is a permeability between conscious experience and the unconscious, a flow of images, emotions, thoughts and body sensations emerging into awareness from within. Jung believed that this permeability is a central factor in the experience of creativity and observed that this is more developed in people who are gifted with creative expression.[145] He located the creative matrix of the unconscious in the archetypal layer of experience. What this means is that there is a vast collection of images and impressions of human experience that becomes accessible when we enter our inner world through self-reflection, attending to dreams, noticing body signals, and developing the capacity for symbolic processing.

We hear quite a bit these days about "emotional intelligence". I am also interested in "symbolic intelligence", the capacity to find meaning and connection with the deeper layers of the psyche. It is symbolic intelligence that allows us to see through the layers of conditioning that would bind us to external rules. When you relocate your reference point to the inner landscape and learn to speak the language of myth and symbol, image and body sensing, you reclaim autonomy.

It may be unfamiliar to think of attending to our internal responses as creative, yet they are events that can result in the creation of new meanings, new possibilities, new perspectives and experiences. This has also been described in many cultural traditions where the experience of insight, healing, discovery, and creativity emerge from an internal process.

In the shamanistic tradition, for example, it is understood that knowledge and insight come from beyond consciousness when the barriers between self and "nonself" become fluid.[146] This is much more about imagination and symbolic processing than intellectual understanding. This also shows up in the therapy process when people have profound intellectual understanding of their life issues but experience no relief or resolution until something breaks through into consciousness from the unconscious. This may happen via a dream or internal focusing or therapeutic intervention that facilitates the permeability between conscious and unconscious.

It was her curiosity about a recurring dream that brought Danielle to therapy. A successful solicitor, healthy and active in her personal life, she announced that she didn't really need therapy but wanted to understand her dream.

> *In the dream she is in a house where she lived in her twenties. She is standing in front of a door she has never seen before and is drawn to open it but experiences a strange reluctance.*

This scene had replayed itself in her dreams five or six times over the preceding year. Thinking about the dream had not brought understanding. The unconscious was presenting a puzzle that could be solved through a rational approach. We did, however, spend several hours talking about what might wait beyond the door, how she might approach it, and whether it was actually important or not, addressing the rational mind concerns about embarking on a strange journey. All of Danielle's questions were like those of a first time diver preparing to enter the depths of the ocean. As she became more trusting of her inner process, Danielle learned to explore her body sense and to attend to other internal responses. She was able to consciously reenter the dream experience, standing by the door. In this way she was able to have an authentic, embodied response to the unknown territory. The mix of excitement and fear she felt each time she approached the door led her to an understanding that she was being called to engage her inner life through more than just intellectual curiosity, and that there were more rooms in the "house" of her psyche than she had ever imagined.

The house of the psyche

The following guided inner journey is based on the idea that the psyche is like a house with many different rooms. We often find ourselves living in one or two rooms and forgetting about the rest of the house. Some rooms are definitely more comfortable than others, yet they all contain aspects of ourselves. There can be cold, bleak rooms where we are stuck at times, or safe spaces deep within the house that are places of healing and restoration.

Discovering the different spaces and even building on or renovating can be an exciting experience.

You can tape the following script or share it with a friend. Take as long as you need exploring the different rooms in the house of your psyche. In the script, I suggest 5 minutes of clock time, but as you become familiar with the process, you can spend as much time as you need in the house of your psyche. You can draw a floor plan or make a model of the house. Some people have met many inhabitants of the rooms and learned about the subpersonalities that live in the psyche. You may encounter a guide or wise inner figure.

Script for inner journey through the house of the Psyche.

Begin by thinking of a place where you feel particularly comfortable and safe; it may be a place in your home, your bedroom for example, or it may be a place in the country or outside somewhere . . .a place where you go often or a place you have only visited once or twice . . .it is only important that this is a place where you can feel safe and comfortable . . . Now I want you to imagine yourself in this place that is safe and comfortable . . .seeing what it is you see when you're in this place . . .hearing the sounds you hear in this place . . .feeling just how it is for you in this place . . .Now take one more look around, seeing the familiar things you see here, and this time I want you to notice something you have never seen before . . .there is a doorway and the door is open . . .and as you move through the door you can look back at any time into the space you

know so well . . .that's right . . .seeing all the familiar things
. . .even as you continue to move deeper and deeper into
this new place you can look back at any time you want and
the door will be open into the place that is safe and
comfortable and known . . .and there up ahead of you in
this new place is a very large expanse of water . . .water as
far as the eye can see . . .and somehow you know that your
journey continues on the other side of this water . . .and
I'm not exactly sure how it is you will find your way across
. . .it may be that you find a way to cross on the surface of
the water . . .or perhaps underneath . . .or somehow
through the air . . .or around . . .but however it is that you
do, you find yourself on the other side . . .continuing to
move deeper and deeper into this new place . . .seeing what
there is to see . . .hearing what there is to hear . . .and
feeling what there is to feel . . .and there up ahead of you is
a building . . .and the door to this place is open also . . .and
as you move inside you notice that whatever it looked like
from the outside it is ever so much larger on the inside . .
.so many rooms . . .so many different spaces . . .and as you
begin to move from room to room . . .from space to space . .
.pay particular attention to the connecting bits . . .the
doorways and passages and hallways and stairways that
allow you to move from space to space . . .from room to
room . . .seeing what there is to see . . .hearing what there is
to hear . . .feeling what there is to feel . . .in this place . .
.continuing to move deeper and deeper into this new place .
. .and somewhere in the centre of this place there is
someone who has been waiting a very long time for you to
arrive . . .take some time now making your way to this
room . . .seeing and hearing and feeling all that is here for
you . . .taking just as much internal time as you need but

about 5 minutes of clock time to move deeper and deeper . . .that's right . . .seeing all there is to see . . .hearing all there is to hear . . .feeling all there is to feel . . .(stop talking here for about 5 minutes) . . .

. . . and knowing that this is a process that will continue in its own way in its own time you can begin now to make the journey back . . .back through these places . . .across to this side . . .back to the space that is familiar and safe and comfortable . . .remembering the way across . . .to the place where you started . . .and from that place to this room . . .the sound of my voice . . .the feeling of your body in the chair . . .allowing your awareness to be fully here . . .opening your eyes.

The shamans in pre-industrial cultures knew about the different "rooms" or states of consciousness that are more or less accessible depending on certain contexts and practices. Modern recreational drug users also know about these different rooms. The difference is that, most of the time, they are taking the journey without the contextual structures that make the difference between idle entertainment and spiritual development.

The shamanistic tradition originated in Paleolithic times and involved the wise ones we now know as witch-doctors, medicine-men, folk healers, and witches.[147] The practices associated with shamanism were usually the result of many years of intensive training and commitment. There have, however, also been reports of spontaneous experiences of healing and discovery that, like the practice of mindbody birth control, have arisen in response to dissatisfaction with available approaches and a conviction that an alternative approach must exist.[148] It is the permeability between conscious and unconscious, and the ability to manage what comes present, that makes this possible.

One of the ingredients of mindbody birth control is a permeability between the conscious and unconscious. What this means is that the inner workings of the psyche are accessible to consciousness. This permeability is also part of the Western magic tradition; magic is sometimes described as the ability to change consciousness at will. Years of working in this tradition with ritual and with the elements of air, fire, water and earth have supported my ability to move between the worlds of conscious and unconscious. One of the invocations in ritual work is that of being *between the worlds, beyond the bounds of time, where night and day, joy and sorrow, birth and death meet as one.* This quintessential expression of permeability reminds me that the experience is not just about me standing in my habitual orientation expecting something to come to me, but rather about finding a place between the worlds where that which is familiar can meet with that which is not yet known. Like Danielle standing at the door she had never seen before, we can decide to enter the experience actively rather than passively waiting for something to happen. This does not mean that we enter our inner world heroically, to overcome or conquer, but rather with a stillness that holds the potential for action, a fundamentally feminine approach to psyche.

So it is with mindbody birth control. The experience is not just about remaining in your habitual orientation and adding another ability. There are doorways and thresholds to cross.

The sort of permeability between conscious and unconscious which makes this practice possible asks for a reorientation, a new perspective. The various practices in this chapter support this shift of perspective, making the crossings possible. The women practising mindbody birth control said "No" to the prevailing beliefs and practices and had to find other ways. They all describe subjective experiences that can best be understood through the elements of creativity:

- an ability to consider new perspectives,

- a permeability between conscious and unconscious,

- concentration and commitment,

- a detachment from the existing forms.[149]

This includes not only a preparedness to separate from certain existing perspectives but also a deep engagement with what is developed to replace them.

Most of the women practising mindbody birth control have described an internal process that requires many hours of sustained immersion and focused concentration. The immersion is described by one woman as an

> *inner process of sensing the ovaries and fallopian tubes and uterus*

and another as

inner process . . .of going into the state of receiving and experiencing something that relates to the question . . .

Some sort of practice involving sustained immersion in internal experience is central to mindbody communication, whether in biofeedback techniques, healing through imagery, or internal regulation of fertility. This sustained immersion has also been called "indwelling", a practice that allows the essential qualities of an experience to reveal themselves from the inside out rather than from the outside in. The body focusing process from Chapter 6 involves this sort of indwelling and supports us to develop permeability between conscious and unconscious.

I am reminded of a time early in my study of academic psychology. Sitting through one more boring lecture at the tender age of 17, I suddenly found myself electrified with excitement when the lecturer started talking about perception. What he was saying is that what we see is not determined by what is out there, nor is it determined by the image received by the visual system; *it is determined by how the information is received and processed inside us.* I knew that I had heard an important truth about my experience of the world.

Practices like sorting the beans, focusing, and other self-reflective exercises are all about noticing what is inside us. There are clinical reports of how the self-observation of a specific response state, such as a phobic response, can produce change in the response[150]. This is what happens in feedback.

Candace Pert has used the metaphor of a helmsman who steers a ship by constantly adjusting the tiller in response to incoming material, or feedback, from sensory information, as an example of a feedback loop.[151] This understanding has been applied in biofeedback, a system of treatment in which patients are trained to modify their own autonomic body processes, especially cardiovascular and respiratory functions. It is equally possible to learn to modify and manage the reproductive system.

This choice to learn conscious regulation was expressed by Katie, a teacher with three children:

> We had a feeling we could go on endlessly, that babies would just keep coming, but that also we were given some degree of choice and that the choice involved responsibility and some consciousness that needs to be part of it.

Working to develop consciousness is a vital part of bringing the Goddess back into our lives.

One way to understand how feedback works is to consider our tendency to assume that a response, especially an emotionally charged response, is the same as our experience of ourselves. We usually say something like, "I am angry" rather than "I am aware of feeling angry" or "my stomach is churning and my heart is beating fast".

When we are identified with a response pattern, it is experienced as automatic and unchangeable.

When we learn to observe what is happening inside, to sort the beans of our response states, and bring them into conscious awareness, we have more choice. Instead of 'this is me" it becomes "these sensations, feelings, thoughts are part of my experience". This allows the possibility of a different relationship with the patterns that have controlled us.

Mindfulness

You can learn to observe your inner experience and move through the rooms in the house of your psyche through the sacred tasks the already described. Another practice that supports this is a meditative or mindfulness practice that comes from the Eastern spiritual tradition. It is a simple practice of counting the breath.

Sit quietly and comfortably somewhere where you will not be disturbed for about twenty minutes. Begin by noticing the breath as it moves in and out. You may feel the air against your nose or moving down into your lungs. Locate a physical experience of the breath.

When you have a physical sense of the breath, begin counting each breath in and out as one: in . . .out . . .one; in . . .out . . .two, and so on up to 10. The start again at one.

If you become distracted or lose count or lose the physical sense of the breath, just start again at one. This is a gentle mindfulness practice that develops your capacity to attend to inner experience.

For some women, the practice of mindfulness needs to begin at an even more fundamental level within the body, as their experience of alienation from themselves is so great that using the breath as a focus proves too elusive.

Finding your own rhythm

Learn to find your own pulse, usually in the wrist, and focus on the rhythm of your own heart beating.

Buy a stethoscope from a medical supplier and spend a few minutes each day listening to your own heart beat.

Your heart beat is a rhythm that is uniquely yours. Women who have heard the sound of their baby's heart beat while still in the womb will remember that it has its own musical cycle, different from the mother's. Listening to your own rhythm offers a deep sense of grounding and reentering embodied experience.

Attending to your pulse by holding your wrist is also something that can be done unobtrusively in a social or work situation to remind you of your own deep inner rhythm at times when it could become lost.

In her translation of ancient Egyptian texts, Normandi Ellis[152], describes the heart connection this way:

> **My heart. My mother. My heart . My mother. My heart of my becoming.**

The ability to develop an internal state of observation supports a practice like mindbody birth control. When you engage the attentional practices, your own inner ground will strengthen. This means you will be more able to separate from conditioned ideas about fertility management and be able to choose a way that works for you. You will also begin to disidentify from previously automatic biological processes and to develop the capacity to regulate them. For most women, the processes of ovulation, fertilisation and implantation seem automatic and uncontrollable. When you develop the inner capacity to observe your experience, these processes are more accessible. Choice and control become possible.

Angela, the woman who encountered her father in her dream preventing her journey to the red waterfall, was able to disidentify from the inner voice that said she did not need to go on the journey to reclaim her wise-blood. This stepping aside and observing allowed her to recognise the obstructing element as an internal masculine energy related to father. Without this disidentification and inner observation, Angela may just have given up and felt defeated, believing herself unable to claim the power of managing her own mindbody process of birth control. Or she may have rationalised that it was a foolish idea anyway. When we cannot find the internal ground to disidentify from inner dynamics, we are unable to make changes, and tend to rationalise our experience in a way that fits with our existing world view.

This experience of witnessing or observing within the participation in our lived experience is very different from observing from outside. It allows you to have an ongoing interaction between experiencing and attending to experience, so that it is a mutual process between mind and body. This mutual process of observing from the inside of an experience involves practices like becoming the womb or talking with an inner figure. This sort of inner work makes intuitive sense to many women who, once again, are just doing this anyway. It can, however, be important to reassure the rational mind that practices like these are not weird and bizarre but have their basis in psychological theories and in traditional approaches to healing the mindbody system.

The idea that matter is something that can respond and interact with us can, however, be difficult to grasp. It is not well understood even in psychology. This is partly because psychological theory often works to objectify experience in order to claim a place in the scientific world. The idea of an active, animate, alive world resonates much more with ancient ways of relating to Nature.

In mindbody birth control, the inner world is active, animate, and alive. A woman's womb calling to be filled (or not) is a very real experience. Mindbody research has now located an enteric brain, an embodied intelligence that we experience as a gut feeling that tells us what is really happening. When we take the time to attend to our bodies, we reconnect with information and wisdom inaccessible to the rational mind. We have all had the experience of ignoring body signals like a full bladder or a rumbling stomach when we become absorbed in some activity. What else are we ignoring when we forget to attend to the body? The following exercise invites participation from within your lived experience.

Shifting perception

You can train yourself to think and perceive differently. This means that you can see the world from outside conditioned forms.

One exercise involves reversing your normal experience.

In the following description, the experience of breathing is reversed so that it is the air doing the breathing:

"I am breathing deeply and slowly in order to summon sleep, and suddenly it is as if my mouth were connected to some lung outside myself which alternately calls forth and forces back my breath"[153]. Experiment with changing your perception:

- Instead of you breathing the air, imagine, sense, feel the air actively wanting to enter your lungs;

- Instead of you reading the words on this page, imagine them actively wanting to enter your eyes and your thoughts.

- Do this at least 3 times each day with everyday experiences like walking, washing the dishes, brushing your teeth etc. Instead of you washing your body, imagine and sense that the water is

washing you; when exercising, imagine and sense that the water in the pool is moving you along, that the running track is moving your feet etc.

Once again, you will discover how your perceptions shape your experience of yourself and the world and have an opportunity to develop the permeability between consciousness and the unconscious that is so necessary for living creatively.

Life is not about mind over matter: mindbody birth control involves one part of me reciprocally interacting with another part of me. It is not about a disembodied me, or mind, acting on body.

By changing your participation in your lived experience, you learn to perceive your mindbody processes as a continuous interchange, a moving back and forth, a reciprocal exchange. As you will see in the next chapter, the flow of information between mind and body is a continuous, two-way interweaving.

I had a delightful dream that brought a spontaneous experience of this sort of reversal of my ordinary waking consciousness,

> *I am travelling with my family. We are stopping at a motel for the night. We are being made welcome as we know someone here. In the middle of the night I am taking care of the two cats we have with us. I am watching an amazing cloud formation through the*

window. There are blue shapes with black and white outlines in an orange/red cloud. It is moving very fast across the sky. I am running for my camera and trying to take pictures through the windows but they are too dirty. I am running outside. The cloud is moving so fast it is breaking up. I am taking pictures. The cloud is going around a group of trees. I am running around the trees and am seeing the last bits of the cloud dissolve into a beautiful tree of blossom. A voice says, 'the tree came into blossom. No! The blossom came into the tree." I am talking with an old woman about the cloud and she is telling me about the shapes in it and about also seeing faces in the tree.

I invite you to take some time to consider these ideas, remembering to breathe and notice your body responses.

Can you imagine the shift from normal everyday perception to an experience of participating in a continuous interchange between mind and body?

Can you imagine the blossom coming into the tree?

The many tasks of psyche suggested here support this sort of experience. The ideas you have encountered here also engage the mystery and integrity of the human experience, offering some explanations and raising important questions about what is possible and how it can happen, while also allowing for the uniqueness of each person's responses.

Psyche made the journey from unconscious absorption to conscious differentiated awareness through engaging the tasks set by the Goddess. The Wayward Princess retained all of her previous experience even while learning to live by new laws that were not determined by her father, the king. When we attend to the inner depths of psyche, we change the balance and learn to live by new laws that emerge from within.

PART IV
MINDBODY/BODYMIND

CHAPTER FOURTEEN

THE MINDBODY CONNECTION

Mindbody birth control is not about mind over matter. It is about the mindbody relationship. It is about getting to know yourself in a different way so that you are not a stranger in your own mindbody systems.

I often suggest that women begin to develop their practice of mindbody birth control by familiarising themselves with the reproductive cycle as we know it from our scientific model of the world. There are many excellent resources for this.[154] It can be useful to look at pictures of the body and diagrams of the reproductive cycle, including the extraordinary live footage of conception now available. It also helps to read about what exactly happens during the cycle. You may find yourself imagining the process of conception and implantation in a particularly individual way. For most of us in the modern world it is, however, the biological model of reproduction that informs our understanding.

The following diagram shows the uterus, ovaries and fallopian tubes in relation to the vagina and the whole pelvic area. Is this how you sense or imagine them to be in your body?

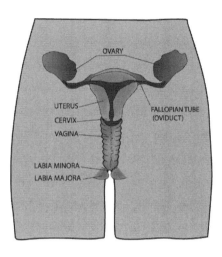

Getting to know your body

Take some time to compare the picture of the reproductive system with your body sense. When you are not pregnant, the uterus is about the size of your clenched fist and rests low in your belly between the bladder and rectum. The area inside, where implantation occurs, is about the size of your thumb, with the walls touching.

Can you imagine or sense the two fallopian tubes? These are about 10cm long and connect from the inside of the uterus to wrap part way around the ovary, extending up

and out of the uterus like the horns won by the Goddess Isis, or like the crescent moon.

Can you locate your ovaries? The ovaries are about the size and shape of a walnut and sit about 10cm below your waist. Can you sense or feel when you ovulate? Some women report distinct body sensations such as slight cramping or mood changes at this time.

Becoming familiar with your cycle can be an important first step in practising mindbody birth control. If you have never done this before, plot your cycle by keeping a diary over three months, marking the first day of your menstrual bleeding, how long it lasts, and noting anything you experience in between. Keep track of your body changes and moods each day by making a few notes or simply drawing a smiling or frowning face to represent how you are feeling on the day. After three months you can trace back fourteen days from the start of your bleeding to find any patterns that occur with ovulation.

Mindbody birth control is not necessarily fixed to the menstrual cycle. It is, however, an embodied process and knowing your own rhythms and cycles helps to ground your practice. By tracking your own cycle in this way, you can also learn to identify the signs that precede menstruation. Anticipating and welcoming the "wise blood" each month is part of the process and is also very affirming.

The human reproductive cycle

The reproductive cycle in the human female is known as the menstrual cycle because the end of each cycle is marked by the bleeding of menstruation, unless pregnancy occurs. Long before there was any understanding of internal mechanisms of the menstrual cycle, this periodic bleeding represented woman's relationship with the cycles of the moon and the changing seasons. Medical science can now describe how the anterior pituitary in the brain stimulates the production of a succession of hormones during the menstrual cycle and how the relative concentrations of these hormones influence the changes in the uterus.

Although the whole process continues in an interactive round, it can be said to start when Gonadotropin-releasing-hormone (GnRH) is released from the hypothalamus in the brain. GnRH stimulates the pituitary gland to produce follicle stimulating hormone (FSH) which stimulates the growth of the follicle and egg in the ovary. This also stimulates the ovary to produce oestrogen which causes the egg to mature in an ovarian follicle and the lining of the uterus to build up in preparation for possible conception.

When the production of FSH falls off, the next hormone produced by the pituitary (luteinising hormone, LH) induces ovulation and the formation of a corpus luteum in the ovary from the burst follicle. A third pituitary hormone (luteotropic hormone, LTH) maintains the corpus luteum and stimulates it to produce progesterone which maintains the wall of the uterus in a suitable state for the embryo.

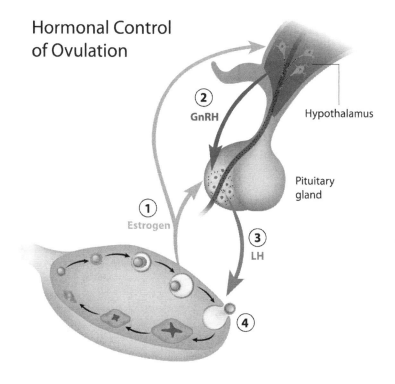

Hormonal Control of Ovulation

This is not a one way process as the changing secretory activity of the pituitary is at least partly influenced by feedback from the ovary. Just as the pituitary secretes FSH at the beginning of the cycle to stimulate the development of the follicle, the growing follicle secretes oestrogen, causing the level of oestrogen in the blood to rise. These higher concentrations of oestrogen inhibit the production of FSH by the pituitary, which switches instead to the production of LH and LTH, thereby inducing ovulation.

While the corpus luteum is developing and continuing to secrete hormones, this continues to suppress the secretion of FSH. If no embryo is implanted in the uterus, the corpus luteum degenerates, the levels of oestrogen and progesterone in the blood fall, and the pituitary starts to produce FSH once more.

Mindbody communication is a two-way process with constant interaction. The practice of mindbody birth control involves an internal process of engaging thoughts, feelings, images and body sensings that are transformed into neurochemical messages and transmitted via the hypothalamic-pituitary axis. The hypothalamus transduces these processes of "mind" into informational substances which communicate with the pituitary gland. The pituitary gland and ovaries also communicate with each other via hormonal messenger molecules. The pathways of this communication can be very direct with informational substances moving not only via the nervous system, but also through blood, cerebrospinal fluid and extracellular space.

To become pregnant, sperm ejaculated from a man's penis must enter into (or very close to) a woman's vagina and travel through the cervical opening, through the uterus and into the fallopian tubes. Sperm and egg must then meet in the outer third of the fallopian tube, where fertilisation occurs when a single sperm unites with the egg. This forms a new bundle of cells, the zygote, that takes several days to travel down the fallopian tube to the uterus. For pregnancy to occur, the zygote must then implant into the uterine wall and continue growing into a baby.

One of the essential ingredients in this process is the woman's fertile mucous. Several days before an egg is released, the mucous glands in a woman's cervix activate, secreting mucous into the vagina. This mucous helps protect the sperm from acidic secretions in the vagina, keeping the sperm alive for several days. This "fertile" mucous also guides the sperm towards the uterus, preparing them for fertilisation. Without this support from the woman's body, sperm die within a few hours. Another essential ingredient is the receptivity of the endometrium or lining of the uterus to the fertilised egg.

Managing fertility

Take some time to consider the elements of this process. There are many points where it can be interrupted. As you can see, it is the woman's body that must be receptive to the sperm, support the meeting of sperm and egg, and allow implantation for pregnancy to occur. It is not determined by the masculine.

Your task is to imagine or sense how you can interrupt or block the process of fertilisation and implantation. Some women have a sense it is possible to make the mucous secretions in the vagina unfriendly to sperm, so that they do not even make it as far as the uterus. Others imagine or sense an obstacle of some kind that blocks the sperm's access to the uterus, or perhaps the fallopian tubes, like the trapdoor in the image in Part II. Some women focus on making the uterine wall inhospitable, so that the zygote cannot implant. There are many variations of these interruptions.

Trust the process that makes sense to you, or work with several stops and interruptions to ensure that your practice of mindbody birth control is thoroughly engaged.

Once you have decided how to approach this, you need to develop a regular practice of visualisation, sensing and internal focused attention. This is described further in the next chapter.

Scientific research and mindbody birth control

What does biological research say about regulating this process through an internal mindbody process? Current scientific research is exploring the area of mindbody communication and can, in fact, describe the sort of psychobiological (mindbody) communication pathways via which mindbody birth control works. This is not, however, a specific area of study in mindbody research. This may well be because the contraceptive Pill seems to take care of birth control and there are more pressing demands from other areas, or it may be that researchers have not even considered the possibility of internal regulation of fertility. The taboo against women assuming full reproductive autonomy is far reaching.

Some years ago, I was supporting a woman who needed urgent medical attention for a genetic disorder involving menstrual bleeding. The doctor told me that little was known about her condition, as women's disorders traditionally received less attention in medical research. While this may be changing, it is likely that this bias still exists. So the connections I am making between current research findings and mindbody birth control are mine, but the links are definitely there to be found.

Psychobiological research can explain the mindbody process that prevents conception for the African woman jumping over a bush, the Aboriginal woman not inviting the spirit of the child to enter, and my experience of internal regulation of fertility.

MIndbody communication

Early researchers thought about the mindbody connection as an interlocking network of informational systems -- genetic, immunological, hormonal, and so on, each with their own language. They were looking for the mechanism that would allow the code of one system to be translated into the code of another system[155].

As early as 1936, there were theories of how mental and/or physical stress was translated into psychosomatic problems by the hypothalamic-pituitary-adrenal axis of the neuro-endocrine system.[156] They were finding pathways by which mind (thoughts and emotions as neural impulses) could communicate with body (hormonal molecules).[157] More recent research has suggested that the mindbody relationship is even more immediate and less separate than these earlier theories indicate.[158]

The endocrine or hormonal system is comprised of many organs located throughout the body, each of which secretes hormones into the bloodstream to regulate cellular metabolic functions such as growth, activity level, and sexuality. It has been established that the pituitary gland at the base of the brain sends out hormones as "messenger molecules" to regulate all the other hormone-producing organs of the body. The pituitary is, in turn, modulated by the limbic-hypothalamic system in the brain, the centre related to emotional regulation. Central to this system is the hypothalamus which acts to pick up information about the internal environment from the blood and cerebro-spinal fluid, and about the external environment from the sense organs. The limbic-hypothalamic system is thought to be the major centre for integrating this information with the processes of mind and then relaying it to the pituitary which regulates all the other organs of the endocrine system.[159]

Since many of the multiple functions of hormones are mediated either directly or indirectly by the limbic-hypothalamic-pituitary system, they are accessible to mind modulation and hypnotherapeutic intervention. In other words, the activity of hormones can be affected by significant life experiences, mental, emotional and physical processes, and this can be encoded in memory, learning, and behaviour.

In relation to mindbody birth control, there is research which shows that progesterone levels are linked to behavioural and psychological responses.[160] Other research has shown that the pituitary hormone, ß-endorphin, is involved in the regulation of LH.[161] What this means is that "mind" can modulate the hormones that directly affect conception. These studies are beginning to explore the close relationship between internal (mind) states and the central nervous system release of bio-chemicals, showing that it is possible to regulate reproductive hormone secretion via endorphin levels; in other words, mindbody birth control.

There have, however, been technical difficulties in closely studying the mindbody links in human reproduction.[162] Research with other mammals has begun to find that the ability to alter the pattern of GnRH stimulation is an essential part of the regulation of reproduction.[163] This is important because GnRH is one of the reproductive hormones that is determined by the activity of the hypothalamus, one of the main links between mind and body.

Another substance closely linked to hypothalamic-pituitary function is known as inhibin and is implicated in regulation of FSH in the menstrual cycle.[164] Inhibin has also been linked to diminished ovarian reserve, one indicator of infertility.[165] What this suggests is that the levels of a substance like inhibin, which can be affected by limbic system activity (emotions, inner work, and other internal state shifts), are involved in a woman's ability to conceive. Research suggests that the levels of a substance like inhibin are regulated via the hypothalamic-pituitary axis, the very pathway by which the messages of mind are translated into the language of body.

Of particular relevance to mindbody birth control is the finding that women with unexplained infertility have subtle disturbances in the hypothalamic-pituitary-ovarian axis compared with fertile women.[166] While this has been studied in relation to infertility, it can, of course, apply as easily to conscious, deliberate infertility as well as involuntary infertility. One of the research papers even comes close to the idea of mindbody birth control, recognising that the effects of compounds such as inhibin could be important in birth control, and suggesting they might form the basis for explaining "novel" contraceptive interventions. They might indeed !

One of the women practising mindbody birth control was describing her experience of reproductive choice:

> *In regulating conception it feels like there are those
> two points: actual acceptance of the sperm by the egg
> then the acceptance by the mother, embedding in the
> uterus.*

If she reframed that into the language of the psychobiologists,
she might say that

> *In regulating conception it feels like there are those
> two points which can be interrupted by altering the
> neuro-endocrine balance in the mindbody system.*

The long history of hypnotherapeutic intervention in menstrual disorders also supports the link between states of mind and reproductive hormones.[167] One of the foremost practitioners of therapeutic hypnosis, Dr. Milton Erickson, reported that menstruation could be skipped, precipitated, interrupted, or prolonged as a function of emotional stress. It has been hypothesised that stress-related distortions in the central nervous system release of ß-endorphin are related to amenorrhoea (lack of menstruation), and perhaps other menstrual disorders such as dysmenorrhoea (painful menstruation) and premenstrual syndrome. While all of these reports are about involuntary (unconscious) experiences of menstrual disruption, they clearly suggest pathways of mindbody communication by which conscious control of these processes can occur.

One branch of psychobiology, psychoneuroimmunology, specifically explores the communication links between the brain and the immune system. These links have been established through experiments that have demonstrated both subconscious and conscious control of the immune system.[168] Using self-regulatory practices such as relaxation, self-hypnosis, imagery, and biofeedback training, it has been found that conscious intervention can directly affect cellular function in the immune system. Biofeedback research has demonstrated that adequate monitoring and rapid feedback makes it possible to control any body function to some extent.[169]

It is, however, the less tangible forms of mindbody communication, such as the use of imagery, which are most relevant to internal regulation of fertility. The role of the imagination in healing suggests a more subtle, yet even more direct, access to mindbody communication pathways.

Progressive relaxation

Progressive relaxation is an internal healing process that involves imagining or sensing the body. This is one of the exercises I learned during my first pregnancy, and have now been practising for thirty years. It is a gentle way of saying "hello" to the whole mindbody system and becoming familiar with how it works.

To engage this process you need about forty minutes of uninterrupted time. Find a comfortable place to sit or lie down in a position in which you will be at ease for the whole time. If you do need to move, do so slowly and mindfully, rearranging your position so that you can continue the process.

This is an invitation to the muscles and cells of the body to release *in their own particular way.* This means that there is no right way or wrong way for the relaxation to happen. Sometimes there may be obvious sensations such as warmth, softening, tingling or other signs of letting go. At other times, the effects may not be obvious at all. Just allow your mindbody system to respond in whatever way is appropriate each time without judging the experience. It can be surprising to find that a progressive relaxation session in which not much seemed to happen can leave you feeling rested and renewed, or at least more familiar with your own mindbody system.

The process simply involves you focusing your attention on each part of the body and saying internally, "My (body part) is releasing. I am relaxing my (body part). My (body part) is releasing". For example: "My toes are releasing. I am relaxing my toes. My toes are releasing." The mindbody system responds to repetition, so just keep saying the same phrase for every body part as you move up to the top of your head.

Remember, this is an invitation and there really is no particular response that has to happen. Just enjoy visiting each part of your body in this way.

Begin the process by noticing your breath as it moves in and out of your body. Then take your attention all the way down to your toes. You may want to move your toes. Just notice your toes and internally invite them to relax and release by saying, "My toes are releasing. I am relaxing my toes. My toes are releasing." Take two or three breaths to

notice how the toes respond to this invitation and then move on to the feet, repeating the words for this part of the body. Move to the next area after two or three breaths.

Repeat this sequence for the lower legs, knees, thighs, pelvic area including buttocks, genitals and hips, lower back, belly area, middle back, abdomen, upper back, chest and breasts, shoulders, upper arms, elbows, forearms, wrists, hands, fingers, neck, face, and scalp. Just say the same words for each body part, remembering to pause for a few breaths to allow time to notice the body's responses.

You can extend your practice to include all of your internal organs, the entire nervous system, and the endocrine glands. If you are not familiar with all of these and where they are located, you can refer to a basic anatomy book like The Anatomy Colouring Book by W Kapit & L M Elson, New York, Harper & Row.

As you become more familiar with your mindbody system, you will recognise signals and communications from all over the body.

Research over the last twenty years has pointed to very direct pathways of mindbody communication. Endocrine hormones have been found to facilitate mindbody communication within the brain itself, not just between brain and body.[170] In particular, the pituitary hormones, endorphins or enkephalins, work in this way in modulating stress, pain, moods, sexuality, and appetite.[171]

One of the pioneers of psychoneuroimmunology, Candace Pert[172], has established that mindbody interaction is even more subtle and complex than the pituitary-hypothalamic model of information transduction. She extends the emotional brain beyond the classical locations in the actual brain to include other areas of the bodymind system. This is the territory of the enteric brain mentioned earlier.

The basic elements of this are "receptor molecules", chemicals that

> hover in the membranes of your cells, dancing and vibrating, waiting to pick up messages carried by other vibrating little creatures . . .which come cruising along - diffusing - through the fluids surrounding each cell . . .they cluster in the cellular membrane waiting for the right chemical keys to swim up to them through the extracellular fluid and then mount them by fitting into their keyholes - a process known as binding.[173]

The chemical key that binds to the receptor, and works to allow information to enter the cell, is called a ligand. Ligands come in three chemical types: neurotransmitters, steroids, and peptides. Peptides are the most numerous and play a wide role in regulating practically all life processes.

It has long been understood that neurotransmitters act by jumping from one neuron to another in the nervous system carrying messages for "on" or "off", telling the cell whether to discharge electricity or not. Peptides, on the other hand, can act like neurotransmitters and can also move through extracellular space in the blood and cerebrospinal fluid, acting even more directly by causing complex changes in the cell whose receptor they lock onto.

Pert performed numerous brain mapping studies of both the peptides and the receptors, discovering that the peptides showed up in areas of the brain as well as in other areas of the body. It is now understood that the peptide network extends beyond the brain to organs, tissue, skin, muscle, endocrine glands, and the autonomic nervous system, and across the endocrine, neurological, gastrointestinal, and immune systems. In fact, many substances previously identified as something else are now understood to be peptides. Pert calls them "informational substances", the true messenger molecules that distribute information throughout the organism.

Inhibin, the substance mentioned earlier, is a peptide. Research is still exploring the precise connections among all parts of the body suggested by peptide activity. In his review of the psychobiology of mindbody healing, Dr. Ernest Rossi presented a vast body of research findings in support of the conclusion that

> there is no mysterious gap between mind and body . .
> .memory, learning, and behaviour processes encoded
> in the limbic-hypothalamic and closely related
> systems are the major information transducers that
> bridge the Cartesian dichotomy between mind and
> body. [174]

Pert says that the pathways through which the conscious mind can affect the unconscious mindbody system are almost infinite.[23]

The complex mindbody relationship that modern science is investigating does, therefore, support the practice of mindbody birth control. This can be reassuring for people who are suspicious of "old wives' tales", mythology and witchcraft. While the scientific connections might be irrelevant for the women who are just doing it anyway, they may be necessary for the practice of mindbody birth control to become accessible to women more generally.

For Annie, a thirty five year old mother of three, who is very committed to mindbody birth control,

> *The no to being pregnant is in the vagina, the stomach, the legs, my whole being does not want to be pregnant. It has to be an embodied experience.*

For me the mindbody birth control practice involved an inner process of sensing the ovaries and fallopian tubes and uterus and saying, *"No baby"*, while imagining the lining falling away and shedding completely.

The subjective experience of controlling conception in this way involves consciously sensing or visualising a biological process and altering this to prevent conception. Whether the focus is on a biological process, on refusing the spirit of the child a home, or on jumping over a bush, it seems that all of these self-regulated birth control methods are working through the mindbody communication pathways now being mapped by psychobiological studies.

One of the learnings from my own research and the studies of anthropology, is that women do not have to be thinking in scientific terms to be effective in this area. When I practise mindbody birth control, I am not attempting to calibrate the exact levels of FSH or GnRH or inhibin in my system. I am simply communicating the "No" as clearly and congruently as I can, with an awareness of connecting to body sensation and imagery. The mindbody system takes care of the rest.

All of the women I spoke with about mindbody birth control talked about the biological process of conception and birth control and showed an understanding of these processes. They did not, however, always consciously use this knowledge in their practice. Some women prefer to explain conception to themselves in other ways and, like the Trobriand Islanders, are just as effective in preventing conception.

There is, then, a meeting place for the teachings and practices from ancient rituals and mysteries, and modern scientific approaches. Perhaps this is an appropriate metaphor for the new consciousness which is being heralded as humanity moves into a new era: a respect and regard for the teachings of mythology and ancient religions, with the leading edge of scientific research to place these in a context that satisfies the rational demands of the contemporary mythology of scientific principles.

To conclusively prove the validity of mindbody birth control in the terms of bio-medical research, there is more hard scientific study to be done; it remains an untested hypothesis in this area. Yet it is an hypothesis based on an ever-increasing foundation of research that is scientifically well documented.

Contemporary science is presenting theories so radical that there is little research to verify or deny their validity. Physics, for example, has adopted a rationale which recognises an inherent connection between observer and observed, suggesting a model of interconnectedness that is consistent with the relationship between psyche and matter described by Pert and discussed in studies of alchemy and Jungian psychology.

I sincerely hope that if and when science turns its attention to mindbody birth control, it will be within the context of the psychological, mythological, and historical perspectives presented in this book. Otherwise, such research could be merely another link in the chain of psychobiological connections, rather than an investigation of true reproductive autonomy for women. As I mentioned before, one of the interesting responses to my research in this area has been the amount of interest by health professionals and researchers in the implications for infertility. There is an obvious extension of this work into the area of infertility. It is, however, significant that this application of mindbody birth control is the one that has been greeted with most enthusiasm when the ideas have been presented to members of the medical profession.

While this may sound like a petty concern in the light of the obvious personal suffering involved in experiences of infertility, there is a broader significance in the fact that medical professional are more interested in correcting infertility than in offering true reproductive autonomy. This needs to be understood in light of the power dynamics discussed in the previous chapters, and the debate surrounding this area raises profound ethical and moral issues.[175]

When women practice true reproductive autonomy, they take back the power of creation from the prevailing fertility power brokers, the drug companies, reproductive and genetic engineering organisations, and Western medical science.

PART V
JUST DOING IT ANYWAY!

CHAPTER FIFTEEN

MAKING IT HAPPEN

As you have seen, the practice of mindbody birth control is something that some women are just doing anyway. It is also something that you can learn to do by making links between thoughts, beliefs, images, emotions, body sensations, and behaviours. We have considered these links from various perspectives and there are many sacred tasks and practices to support you in developing your own relationship with birth control according to the Goddess.

Think of the story of *The Wayward Princess*. Whether this story is interpreted from the perspective of inner dynamics or as a parable about power dynamics in the world, it is a story of choice vs no choice, control vs no control, and empowerment vs disempowerment, the themes that consistently emerge in the story of women's experience of fertility management. Remember when I talked about the psychologist, Abraham Maslow? He would have recognised both the wayward princess and her many times great grandmother, Lilith, as demonstrating autonomy and resistance to enculturation. They also demonstrate pro-active choice, control and empowerment, the very qualities described by women practising conscious mindbody birth control.

The mythic stories are metaphors for the experience of true reproductive autonomy. In developing my practice of mindbody birth control, I moved from dependency on conventional methods to the recognition that these methods did not hold absolute rightness for me, to an active search for alternative approaches that would allow me true reproductive autonomy. This is also obvious in the statements about dissatisfaction with conventional methods and the clear determination to have no more children that have motivated other women to develop an alternative birth control practice. Like Lilith and the wayward princess, they said "No" to the prevailing order and "No" to being disadvantaged by this.

Obviously dissatisfaction with conventional methods of birth control is not a sufficient motivation to develop mindbody birth control. This dissatisfaction was widespread among the women I spoke with, with many reports of powerlessness and lack of choice in birth control. The difference between the women using mindbody birth control and those continuing to practise a method with which they were not satisfied must, therefore, rest with something other than the experience of dissatisfaction and powerlessness.

Women who practice mindbody birth control have also taken the step of actively seeking an alternative practice that meets their values of choice, control and empowerment. The element that I have called "ruthlessness" seems to be one component of this next step; the clear and unequivocal decision to have no (more) babies. However, this determination to not have a child is not exclusive to women practising mindbody birth control, nor is the active search for viable alternative methods of birth control. It seems that these are necessary but not sufficient elements to explain this experience.

The story of the wayward princess offers a fuller explanation of conscious mindbody birth control. In combination with the strong desire to stop conceiving, there is also the belief that something other than conventional "laws" must be possible. This is one of the things that makes the women practising mindbody birth control different from many other women who also feel dissatisfied with conventional methods, who value choice and control, and have a desire to find viable alternative practices. There is, therefore, a combination of elements that emerges for women practising conscious mindbody birth control:

- they are dissatisfied with conventional birth control methods;

- they value choice, control and empowerment;

- they are ruthless in their determination to have no more children;

- they are actively seeking a viable alternative method of birth control;

- **they believe this to be possible outside the existing forms.**

The experience of mindbody birth control is a creative impulse arising from instinctual wisdom in response to a conscious commitment to find a new approach. Like the wayward princess, the women practising this had said "No" to the prevailing laws and believed that they could find other laws by which to live.

They describe experiences that reflect the process of creativity:

- an ability to consider new perspectives,

- a capacity to see beyond the obvious to new possibilities,

- a permeability between the conscious and unconscious,

- concentration, commitment, and deep engagement.

We can, then, see that the women practising mindbody birth control methods

- **value choice, control and empowerment in fertility management;**

- **are ruthless in their determination to have no more children;**

- **are actively seeking a viable alternative method of birth control;**

- ASSUME THIS IS POSSIBLE OUTSIDE THE EXISTING FORMS;

- EXPERIENCE A PERMEABILITY BETWEEN THE CONSCIOUS AND UNCONSCIOUS;

- APPROACH THE ALTERNATIVE PRACTICE OF BIRTH CONTROL WITH CONCENTRATION AND COMMITMENT.

It is the *combination* of all of these elements that makes mindbody birth control possible.

Women's stories tell us that mindbody birth control is an experience that emerged for each woman according to the sensations, emotions, images, symbols, and words that made sense to her. Hence the different emphasis on bodily processes and spirituality, for example. As anthropology so clearly demonstrates, there are many different ways to make sense of the world of experience. Research into systems of healing that incorporate mindbody processes has demonstrated that the images, symbols, and ideas that work best are those which have meaning for the person.[176] It is, therefore, not sensible to generalise from the specifics of any one woman's description of her experience of internal regulation of fertility.

You need to develop your own relationship with the contraceptive process and find a unique, creative response to this. The first step is making a commitment to this as an ongoing study, doing the sacred tasks and practices regularly, and gathering information through self-observation and self-reflection.

If attention is directed to *what* it is that the women practising mindbody birth control are doing, the most rational explanation comes from psychobiological research into mindbody communication. In order to learn mindbody control of fertility, however, it is necessary to focus attention on *how* women are doing this. The specific sacred tasks described in this book all address this. They develop the capacities necessary to develop a successful practice of mindbody birth control. While most of the exercises are not about birth control per se, they focus attention on inner experience and the mindbody process.

My own experience and the different approaches described by other women suggests that you must begin by developing relationship with your mindbody system and with your own personal mythology about birth control. This necessarily involves sorting through the conditioned learnings and attitudes, just as Psyche sorted the beans and seeds for the alchemical Goddess.

Some sort of practice involving sustained immersion in internal experience is central to mindbody communication, whether in bio-feedback techniques, healing through imagery, or internal regulation of fertility. Throughout this book there are practices that you can use to deepen the connection between conscious awareness and the unconscious aspects of psyche. Think of these as the tasks set for you by the Goddess, so that you, like Psyche, can develop the consciousness that allows choice and autonomy.

DOING IT!
PRACTISING MINDBODY BIRTH CONTROL

While all of the tasks in this book make up the ground of mindbody birth control, there are certain specific steps in developing your practice.

1. It is important to examine your intention to have no children, or no more children, for the time you engage this practice. Is this just a vague idea or is it a considered decision and a deeply felt knowing? You may need to discuss this and write down all the reasons why a baby is not wanted at this stage.

The natural desire to conceive is a strong force and tasks like focusing and self-dialogue are valuable at this stage to determine the motivations that make up your experience of conceiving/not conceiving. The clear intention to not become pregnant is an essential first step in this process. Some women say that this ruthlessness is clearer after having at least one child. There have, however, been women with no children who have successfully practised mindbody birth control. The exercises in Chapter 6 can help you sort through the beliefs that may influence your decision.

Once you have made this decision, you can take two or three moon/menstrual cycles before beginning to use mindbody birth control to track your internal responses, engaging self-dialogue, focusing on body parts and emotions, and recording dreams. It is important to negotiate complete agreement within your system about the intention to not conceive..

2. Explore your understanding of reproduction. Study the pictures in Part IV. Think about it, wonder about it, consider it from different perspectives (from the perspective of the ovary, the egg, the sperm etc.). Actually make a workbook for this stage of your practice. Begin to develop an impression of where and how this process can be interrupted for you. This is different for different people. Some possibilities include:

- imagining or sensing a barrier that prevents the sperm from entering the womb or entering the fallopian tubes where conception actually occurs;

- a sperm unfriendly vaginal environment;

- a uterine wall that blocks implantation, or is not receptive to offering the fertilised egg a home in which to develop;

- saying "No" to the spirit of the being who wants to enter.

These interventions can be visual (seen as internal images), auditory (heard as internal sounds/voices) and/or kinaesthetic (sensed in the body). Using all three modalities is always more powerful. The individual nature of this process becomes obvious when you consider the variety of images and interventions that have emerged for women developing their practice of mindbody birth control:

- imagined and sensed plastic caps that prevent sperm from entering the cervix

- red velvet curtains or trapdoors that open and close to regulate conception

- saying "No" to the spirits of potential babies

- saying "No" to implantation.

- bringing on menstrual bleeding when it is due

You may be surprised and delighted by the images and ideas that occur to you as you engage this stage of your practice. There is no right way or wrong way to find the point(s) of intervention. The variety of images and methods developed by the women with whom I have spoken has convinced me that this stage of developing the actual internal practice must be particular to each woman, arising from her own bodymind processes. Your mindbody birth control practice has to make sense to <u>you</u>.

3. Develop a regular practice that incorporates the specific processes that come to you for interrupting and preventing conception. Central to this practice is the image, visual, auditory and/or sensing process that is your personal way of stopping conception and/or implantation. This can become a simple internal practice that only takes a few minutes of concentrated focus. Initially you can practice this daily, or several times a day, gradually reducing the conscious practice as the process becomes deeply embedded in your mindbody system. Some people practice their method each time they have sexual contact. Others intensify their practice around the time they expect to menstruate. Others engage the practice every night before going to sleep. It's up to you. When in doubt, do all of the above until you feel more confident.

When I first developed my practice of mindbody birth control, I used an internal process of sensing my fallopian tubes and uterus as well as seeing them in my mind's eye. I imagined, both visually and kinaesthetically, the fertilised egg being refused a place to implant. The actual refusal took the form of an auditory injunction of "No baby!" that I said internally while sensing the movement of the fertilised egg down the fallopian tube and sensing the shedding of the lining of the uterus so that there would be no home for the fertilised egg.

At first, I did this whole process every time I was sexually engaged with my partner and many times in between as well, especially around the time I expected to menstruate. As I became more confident, I only did it when I felt at particular risk of pregnancy. Some of the signals for me that I needed to attend more closely were particular emotional states that I associate with wanting a baby, particular relationship dynamics, and certain body sensations that simulate early pregnancy. For many years until menopause, I only consciously engaged the process once or twice a year. I have, however, consistently practised the exercises described in this book. I do this to ensure that I am as conscious as I can be in my relationship with my mindbody system, with the emotions, beliefs, body and mood states, and the archetypal energies that can affect not only birth control practice, but also the way I live my life.

For the first few cycles, you may want to engage your specific practice as well as using condoms or withdrawal during your fertile times. You need to build your confidence with mindbody birth control in your own time.

4. Keep a record of your menstrual cycle and increase your practice around the time your period is due. Anticipate the bleeding. Get to know the way your body feels as you are about to menstruate. Take note of the mood changes and internal states that signal menstruation. When you are familiar with these you can encourage them to be present through internal focusing, imagination and visualising processes.

Remember to keep these embodied so that the experience is connected. It will probably not work to just wish that your period would come. You need to feel the body sense, smell the blood and be inside the mood state of menstruating, as if it is actually happening right now. So that rather than thinking about it, you are taking yourself into the actual embodied experience of it.

5. Welcome the menstrual bleeding. This may sound obvious but, once again, you may encounter generations of conditioning that make you ambivalent about menstruating. Develop your relationship with the deep feminine mystery of the "wise blood".

6. Consider your attitudes to an unwanted pregnancy. The "ruthlessness" of refusing the fertilised egg a home in which to grow, or of saying "No" to the spirit of a child who wants to enter is one aspect of mindbody birth control. This attitude is also consistent with choosing assisted abortion. If you were to become pregnant, is abortion an option you would consider? If not, what are your concerns? This can be an important area for discussion and self-reflection as it can highlight reservations about assuming full reproductive autonomy.

When Karen became pregnant while developing her mindbody birth control practice, she was comfortable with choosing to have an abortion. She was determined in her decision to claim 100% responsibility for her reproductive choices and experienced the abortion as a part of this. As she said, *Whichever way it happens, I can't lose.* Her clear intention was to not have another baby. Obviously Karen does not want to use this option regularly, but she also realises that mindbody birth control takes practice and a willingness to learn from experience.

If this story disturbs you, take some time to consider what your response would be to becoming pregnant while developing your practice of mindbody birth control. Just like any other approach to birth control, this method will only work when it is practised thoroughly, with rigorous attention to the internal elements that affect reproductive choice. There are many factors that affect this:

- deeply conditioned beliefs about assuming reproductive autonomy,

- shame based responses to reproductive processes, especially unwanted pregnancy,

- fluctuations in mood states,

- changing emotional needs from day to day.

The practice of mindbody birth control is a serious commitment to consistent inner work. It takes courage and persistence to discover, as the wayward princess did, that we can live according to our own laws.

7. Sharing this process with other women can offer support and endorsement. You can reinforce each others' intentions to prevent conception in this way and support each other through times of doubt or fear. Educating each other about the historical and political aspects of reproductive autonomy can help with examining and stepping aside from conditioned beliefs and responses. You can do this by organising a women's consciousness raising group where these issues are discussed or perhaps a support group or a moon ritual group as suggested in Part III. Whatever the reason for your gathering, there is power in meeting together to reclaim women's ways.

PART VI

DREAMING THE DREAM ON

CHAPTER SIXTEEN
WHAT NOW?

When a baby is growing in a woman's womb, the mother-to-be is not only supporting and nourishing the development of her child's body. She is also dreaming her baby into being, spinning and weaving the basic fabric of the life that is forming. In this same way, the Mother of us all dreamt us into existence, spinning and weaving the mysterious wonders of life. Just as we can learn to attend to the dreams that come to us in the night, we can also find our way back to this original dream of the Mother.

This reconnection is currently happening in many ways, through literature, art, discoveries in various fields of science, through environmental and ecological awareness, and through mindbody healing techniques. It is also happening as women's mysteries, lost for so long in the socio-cultural transitions of our history, are finding their way back into consciousness, restoring something of the original dream of the Mother of us all.

This is a dream of cyclical return, of changing seasons, changing ages. The seasonal observations of the Goddess religions with their veneration of the cycles of death and rebirth in Nature are very different from the doctrines of the patriarchal religious and scientific traditions. The Goddess dreams a dream of eternally returning, a dream of renewable creative experience, personally and collectively. The Goddesses with their wise blood and moon cycles are better guides to sustaining life on this planet than the current philosophies of the masculine principle.

Rediscovering and reclaiming birth control according to the Goddess is one way She is reentering our lives. It seems clear to me that the practice of mindbody birth control is not just a remembering of a forgotten historical practice; it is also one of the signs of a new consciousness that incorporates a deep reverence for the creative energy of the universe.

We are truly alive in interesting times. Interesting because we are alive as one age shifts into the next. Interesting because so many people in so many disciplines are being called to examine the ways in which human beings experience reality and to question the premises on which "reality" rests. Things are not what they seem.

The assumptions of the age of rational consciousness are being challenged in both science and religion. What if Plato was actually constructing reality as he went along rather than basing his philosophy on a long and trusted tradition? What if Descartes was simply trying to make a distinction between spirit and matter and did not intend the absolute and catastrophic severing of mind and body that has since occurred? What if the foundations of our way of thinking and perceiving were formed by young men inventing new realities to explain the natural world? What if the Church destroyed anyone or anything that opposed the orthodox view in their long ago purges, so that we have been left with only one part of the story?

What if things are not what they seem?

If things are not what they seem, we have to do some strenuous work to rediscover an authentic experience of being human. Thankfully, there are many people doing this work and offering it to the world, weaving a tapestry of remarkable richness from our ancient past, and suggesting new possibilities for the future. I have been inspired by these people as I have worked to bring this book to life. This is a book about the present and the ancient past, about rediscovering a way of being that I am sure once existed but was lost along with so much else as the so called civilised world changed from magic and mystery to rationality.

I am writing about birth control as I believe it was practised by women before the takeover of women's ways by church and state powers. This is also something that women are now rediscovering along with the Goddess in her many forms. Mindbody birth control is a birth control practice that restores power to women and offers true reproductive autonomy, a very practical example of the connection between reclaiming women's mysteries and restoring our bond with the rhythms and cycles of nature. If we are to survive even another 100 years, we need this connection to inform the new consciousness that is emerging as we embark on a new century.

Yet this book is about so much more than birth control. It is about living with the Goddess. It is a guidebook for women in this New Age.

It is my hope that more and more women find, like the wayward princess, that they cannot be obedient to laws that have been determined for them by cultural-historical mythologies. I hope that you discover, in the wilderness of your own mindbody system, a life that, as the wayward princess found,

> has a climate and way of existing of its own . . . whose elements belong together, form a completeness, yet neither individually nor collectively do they obey the commands of . . .

the culture, or of scientific and spiritual traditions that do not respect the life-giving power of women, the earth, and Nature.

SHEELA NA GIG
An image for life . . .

177

Above the portals of churches and castles in Great Britain can be found the figurative carving of a Sheela na Gig, a naked woman spreading her legs to display an exaggerated vulva.

Jungian analyst, M Esther Harding, describes this image as " . . . the psychic counterpart or image of the sexual instinct, which Jung called the archetype."[178]

What is the Sheela na Gig showing us?

The vulva or yoni is associated with the mother archetype as a symbol of fertility and fruitfulness.[179] The mother archetype was at the centre of ancient mythologies based on eternal cycles of change and renewal that guided cultures for millennia. These ancient mythologies were profoundly different from the resurrectionist philosophies of the patriarchal religious traditions. Edward Whitmont[180] and others have convincingly argued that the cultural myth of a supreme male deity is losing its ability to guide humankind's collective fate. The myth of the eternal return with the immanence of the sacred in the everyday is more consistent with sustainable, renewable creative experience, personally and collectively.

The Sheela na Gig is a female figure wantonly exposing her vulva to remind visitors of the true meaning of the threshold: a crossing between the worlds. Her presence signals that it is no ordinary crossing; her open vulva defies fondly held beliefs, ideas, and creeds, challenging the assumptions that determine how people live.

As you have seen, any view of reality is filled with these assumptions. Canadian literary critic, Northrup Frye, uses the phrase "mythological conditioning" to describe how the myths by which we live are made up of unconscious beliefs that become regarded as facts.[181] These "facts" then determine experience according to the prevailing mythological conditioning.

Edward Whitmont has described the current time as a low point of "scientific materialism, religious nihilism and spiritual impoverishment"[182].

Jung has warned us that:

> "The world today hangs by a thin thread, and that thread is the psyche of man."[183]

Cultural philosophers have emphasised the inherent difficulty of fully realising a possibility or consciousness beyond the prevailing "facts".[184] The difficultly lies in the tenacity with which human beings hold to their belief systems and assumptions.

Observations at the Harvard-Smithsonian Centre for Astrophysics have demonstrated that even the brightest students in the class have false ideas based on enduring misconceptions that traditional instructional methods cannot overcome. They concluded that

> Until you confront your "private universe" you cannot develop true understanding...[185]

Kurt Lewin, founder of social psychology, developed a practice he called "unfreezing", a process of disconfirming a person's former belief system by examining fondly-held assumptions about self, others, and the world. Lewin, however, found that:

> "Disconfirming information is not enough . . .because we can ignore the information, dismiss it as irrelevant, blame the undesired outcome on others or fate, or, as is most common, simply deny its validity. In order to become motivated to change, we must accept the information and connect it to something we care about."[186]

But this is not easily done.

As Jung says, "the forms we use for assigning meaning are historical categories that reach back into the mists of time . . ."[187]

Even if it is possible to unravel the historical forms, there must also be a tolerance for new information and for the disorientation and discomfort that is inevitably stirred as existing personal, family, and cultural myths are challenged. Human beings have a built in mechanism that defends against information that might disturb homeostasis (consider the futility of good intentions or New Year's resolutions).

Lewin found that change requires taking in and responding to new information that produces an emotional response. This may be experienced as excitement, enthusiasm, or as passion for a cause, and it can also be felt as an uncomfortable dissonance or unease. Most people tend to avoid the unease so that the critical threshold to new experience or understanding is not crossed.

Perhaps they have never encountered the Sheela na Gig!

Being confronted with a naked woman spreading her legs to expose an exaggerated vulva is almost certain to stir excitement, passion, unease, or uncomfortable dissonance.

If the Sheela na Gig was to wear clothes and speak her truth in words rather than image, she might say: "Shed the assumptions that you have inherited from centuries of rational thought and conditioning, and open to the possibility of new experience and meaning."

The Sheela na Gig can help by shocking us out of the conditioning that perpetuates myths of duality and division between body and mind, spirit and matter, the above and the below. She can help us to see through the myths, symbols, and images that have guided humanity to the present time. Then it becomes possible to discern the portals to the sacred that await in dreams, body sensing, images and symbols.

If the Sheela na Gig is effective in her confrontation, a permeability opens between conscious experience and the unconscious, allowing a flow of images, emotions, thoughts and body sensations to emerge into awareness from within. A vast collection of images and impressions of human experience becomes accessible through self-reflection, attending to dreams, noticing body signals. Developing this symbolic intelligence builds the capacity to find meaning and connection with the deeper layers of the human experience, to discover the portals to the sacred.

Remember that in the shamanistic tradition, it is well understood that knowledge and insight come from beyond consciousness when the barriers between self and "nonself" become fluid[188]. This occurs when one is prepared to shift from the habitual to find a place "between" where that which is familiar can meet with that which is not yet known, a liminal state.

The liminal state is named from Latin *limen:* boundary or threshold. Elaborated by anthropologist, Victor Turner, in his studies of pre-industrial rituals and rites of passage, the liminal state is characterized by ambiguity, openness, and indeterminacy.[189] It is a period of transition, during which normal limits are relaxed, opening the way to something new. It is also a time of disorientation, when one's sense of identity and identification with external structures dissolves to some extent. It makes sense that the Sheela na Gig was traditionally placed above the threshold.

Liminality and permeability relate to immanence, that which is indwelling or inherent, "pervading the universe"[190], incorporating the world of Nature. Conversely, transcendence is that which is beyond, "not realisable in experience" or "not subject to the limitations of the physical universe"[191]. How do immanence and transcendence coexist?

Four thousand years ago, in the great river valleys of the East, astronomers and mathematicians searched the Heavens for signs of change. Observing the cycles of the Moon and Venus's flirtatious dance with the Sun, they formulated a relationship between the above and the below. The nature of this relationship has occupied theologians, philosophers, artists, poets, farmers, sailors, and myriad star gazers ever since.

Two thousand years ago, at the commencement of the Piscean Age, an alchemical text called *The Emerald Tablet of Hermes Trismegistus* appeared somewhere in the Middle East. A full translation of one line reads "What is the above is from the below and the below is from the above."[192] From this comes the oft-quoted maxim: "As above, so below".

By splitting the sentence and deleting the balance, rational thought has split the above and the below, separating transcendence and immanence into opposites, dividing and scattering things that may not actually be separate at all.

In Western culture this is evident in the division between mind and body (matter/mater and spirit), where mind is "higher" than body, and the centre of identity is located in our thoughts.

The poet, DH Lawrence, was playing with this in *Demiurge:*

> Even the mind of God can only imagine
> those things that have become themselves;
> bodies and presences, here and now, creatures with a
> foothold in creation ...
> Religion knows that Jesus never was Jesus
> till he was born from a womb, and ate soup and bread
> and grew up, and became, in the wonder of creation, Jesus,
> with a body and with needs, and a lovely spirit.

It is not just poets who have described mind and body, spirit and matter, as two aspects of a single, inter-connected reality[193].

Bio-medical research has revisioned the mindbody relationship as reciprocally interconnecting systems operating with their own intelligences.[194]

Anthropologist, Gregory Bateson[195], clearly describes the fundamental epistemological error of rational consciousness: attempting to understand human processes according to simple causal, mechanistic models.

In a similar vein, biological scientist, Gerald Edelman[196], describes "mind" as the selective coordination of patterns of interconnections between neuronal groups, forming a dynamic loop reminiscent of "entangled" quantum states.

In Bateson's words, "the total system is a sort of a ladder, interlocking settings which are calibrations, which are qualitative, discontinuous, fixed, structural sort of things".[197] Echoes of the spiral markings on the pavements of Irish grave barrows!

Just as mind and body can be experienced as reciprocally connected parts of one system, immanence and transcendence can also be approached as two aspects of a single, inter-connected reality. This is not a blurring of distinctions, but a recognition of the profound interconnectedness of spirit and matter: *What is the above is from the below and the below is from the above.*

The key to this recognition lies in the mystery of perception. Using sight as an example: what one sees is not determined just by what is out there; what one sees is not determined just by the signals that reach the retina of the eye, or the visual cortex in the brain; what one sees is determined by the complex interaction or relationship between the physical environment, the neuronal, muscular and biochemical responses of the body, and the meaning making parts of the mindbody system. In the same way, the experience of immanence and transcendence involves a complex relationship between matter and spirit, with neither being privileged over the other.

Human beings do not have to subscribe to a disembodied, transcendent spirituality to experience a sense of the sacred. Nor does a focus on the everyday stuff of life have to leave us with an experience of "nothing but" matter.

The Sheela na Gig is there to remind us that rational, cognitive processing is not more important than imagination or dreaming or desire.

She is there to remind us that the profane and the sacred exist alongside each other in cyclical interconnectedness.

She is there to locate human experience in the eternal cycles of change that have guided cultures since the beginning of time.

She is there to lead us through the portals to the sacred so we can restore the original dream of the mother of us all, the Earth . . .

ABOUT THE AUTHOR

I write fiction and non-fiction that asks "What if . . .?"

That question lies at the heart of my writing and my life. Things are not always as they seem, and there is so much we don't yet know.

I write to explore possibilities and to invite you between the worlds, beyond the bounds of time . . .

In both my fiction and non fiction writing, I explore possibility. Whether creating alternative worlds or exploring creative alternatives for this world in which we live, I am inspired by magic, mystery, and the spirit that is indwelling in all things.

Don't Take it Lying Down has emerged from my work as a Soul Centred Psychotherapist and from my PhD research.

As well as my non-fiction writing, I have written and published short stories, won some writing prizes, and completed a fantasy trilogy (The Element Series) and an historical/speculative novel (Daughters of Time). Always the theme is "What if . . .?"

I live in a rambling home in south-eastern Australia, with ample walls for my books and murals and a leafy garden for the elements.

Questions and comments welcome
kaalii@kairoscentre.com
http://kaalii.wix.com/soulstory

REFERENCES AND NOTES

CW - <u>The Collected Works of CG Jung</u>, 1953 - 1979, trans. RFC Hull, ed. H Read, M Fordham, G Adler, W McGuire, Bollingen Series XX, Princeton, NJ, Princeton University Press, vols. 1-17.

---

[1] This statue was created in the 13th Century and is located at the entrance portal of the Notre Dame cathedral in Paris.

[2] M Stone, 1978, <u>When God Was a Woman</u>, New York, Harcourt Brace Jovanovich.

[3] G Davis, 1974, <u>Interception of Pregnancy: Post-conceptive Fertility Control</u>, Sydney, Australia, Angus & Robertson, p. 220.

BG Walker, 1983, <u>The Women's Encyclopaedia of Myths and Secrets</u>, New York, Harper & Row, p. 104.

[4] HK Cargill, 1999, <u>A Phenomenological Investigation of a Psychobiological Method of Birth Control</u>, Doctoral thesis held at Monash University, Clayton, Victoria, Australia. Interviews with Australian women practising mindbody birth control.

M Jackson & T Teague, 1978, <u>Mental Birth Control</u>, Oakland, CA., Lawton-Teague Publications.

J Parvati, 1978, <u>Hygieia: A Woman's Herbal</u>, Monroe, UT, Freestone Innerprizes;

A Rosenblum, 1976, <u>The Natural Birth Control Book</u>, Philadelphia, PA, Aquarian Research Foundation;

M Sjoo & B Mor, 1987, <u>The Great Cosmic Mother: Rediscovering the Religion of the Earth</u>, San Francisco, Harper & Row.

[5] Cargill, op. cit., pp. 215-248.

My doctoral research involved three stages of data gathering, analysis and review. As much as it is possible in research, I really did want to find out what might be going on, rather than trying to prove something. There were two stages of language analysis of interview transcripts from five women describing their experience of practising mindbody birth control and five women describing their experience of practising conventional birth control. In the third stage, I used a statistical procedure called Q-sort analysis to find the main factors in women's subjective experience of birth control practices generally. I used fifty verbatim statements selected from all 10 interviews to represent the patterns which were revealing themselves. Thirty women then spent about one hour each organising the statements according to their own experience. This was quite an involved task that went beyond simple question and answer type studies in order to reveal some of the underlying elements in women's experience.

[6] L Kenton, 1995, Passage to Power: Natural Menopause Revolution, Random House, London.

As well as an excellent workbook for menopause, there is information about the dangers of undermining the natural oestrogen/progesterone balance in the body and in the environment.

[7] T Kuhn, 1962, <u>The Structure of Scientific Revolutions,</u> University of Chicago Press, Chicago.

One of the most influential historians of science, Thomas Kuhn has described how objective, impersonal scientific facts can be understood as belief systems which, although true, are not an expression of absolute truth. In other words, just because something can be shown to be true, it does not mean that it is the only truth, or the only way to make sense of our experience. From this perspective, science is just another mythology, and the so called facts of our own time and place may, indeed, be similar to the 'superstitions" of another time and place. In my studies, I have discovered both facts and superstitions that help to explain the idea and experience of mindbody birth control and birth control more generally.

[8] C Spretnak, 1993, Critical and constructive contributions of eco feminism, in P Tucker & E Grim, eds., <u>Worldview and Ecology</u>, Philadelphia, PA, Bucknell Press, pp. 181-189.

[9] Davis, op. cit., pp. 220-221.

[10] I C de Castillejo, 1973, <u>Knowing Woman</u>, New York, G P Putnam's Sons, p. 92.

[11] C B Pert, 1997, <u>Molecules of Emotion: Why You Feel the Way You Feel</u>, New York, Scribner, p. 222.

As well as the exciting mindbody information in this book, Candace Pert shares her journey as a woman working in a scientific community with its bias for the masculine principle.

[12] AR Damasio, 2000. Descarte's Error: Emotion, Reason and the Human Brain. New York, Quill.

[13] C G Jung, CW.

[14] Pert, op. cit.
E L Rossi, The Psychobiology of Mind-Body Healing: New Concepts of Therapeutic Hypnosis, 1988, New York, WW Norton.

[15] JS Bruner, 1964, The conditions of creativity, in Contemporary Approaches to Creative Thinking, ed. HE Gruber, New York, Atherton Press, p. 3.

[16] A Watts, 1968, Myth and Ritual in Christianity, Boston, Beacon Press, pp. 7-8.

[17] N Wolf, 2002, The Beauty Myth: How Images of Beauty are used against Women. New York: Perennial. p.10.\

[18] W I Thompson, 1981, The Time Falling Bodies Take to Light: Mythology, Sexuality and the Origins of Culture. New York, St Martin's Press, p. 165.

[19] Idries Shah in SB Perera, 1986, The Scapegoat Complex: Toward a Mythology of Shadow and Guilt, Toronto, Canada, Inner City Books, pp. 106 -108.

[20] N Wolf, Op. Cit., p.10.

[21] National Health and Medical Research Council, 2000. Post Natal Depression: A systematic review of published scientific literature to 1999.. Commonwealth of Australia.

[22] United Nations Population Fund (UNFPA), 2004, www.unfpa.org/geneder/trafficking.htm

[23] M Gimbutas, 1982, The Goddesses and Gods of Old Europe: 6500-3500 BC, Myths and Cult Images, London, Thames & Hudson Ltd.
Gimbutas has said that the term "Palaeolithic Venus", by which the earliest, small ancient female figurines were first characterised by scholars, is an ironic misnomer. They are not, in fact, representations of an ancient Aphrodite but of the Great Mother.

[24] M Gimbutas, 1991, 'the 'monstrous venus'' of prehistory: Divine creatrix'', in In All Her Names: Explorations of the Feminine in Divinity, eds. J Campbell & C Muses, New York, Harper San Francisco, p. 27.

[25] ibid. p.30.

[26] MR Dexter, 1990, Whence the Goddesses: A Source Book, New York, Pergamon Press.
    R Eisler, 1988, The Chalice and the Blade: Our History. Our Future, San Francisco, Harper & Row.
    M Eliade, 1965, The Two and the One, New York, Harper & Row.

E Neumann, 1991, <u>The Great Mother</u>, Princeton, NJ, Princeton University Press.

M Stone, 1979, <u>Ancient Mirrors of Womanhood: A Treasury of Goddess and Heroine Lore from Around the World</u>, Boston, Beacon Press.

EC Whitmont, 1982, <u>Return of the Goddess</u>, Guernsey, Great Britain, The Guernsey Press.

[27] SN Kramer, 1979, <u>From the Poetry of Sumer: Creation, Glorification, Adoration</u>, Berkeley, CA, University of California Press.

D Wolkstein & S N Kramer, 1983, <u>Inanna, Queen of Heaven and Earth: Her Stories and Hymns from Sumer</u>, New York, Harper & Row.

The written tales, legends, and songs of the ancient Sumerians are a vast body of literature inscribed on clay tablets and fragments dating back to 2000 BC. Folklorist, Diane Wolkstein and cuneiformist, Samuel Noah Kramer, collaborated to tell one of the most ancient stories of the goddesses of birth, life, death, and regeneration.

[28] BD Meador, 1992, <u>Uncursing the Dark: Treasures From the Underworld</u>, Wilmette, IL, Chiron Publications, p. 43.

[29] <u>Larousse Encyclopaedia of Mythology</u>, 1968, London, Hamlyn Publishing Group,   p. 37.

[30] BG Walker, 1983, <u>The Woman's Encyclopaedia of Myths and Secrets</u>, New York, Harper & Row, p. 629.

[31] JG Frazer, 1922, The Golden Bough, New York, Macmillan.

[32] Walker, op. cit., p. 635.

[33] M Stone, 1978, When God Was a Woman, New York, Harcourt Brace Jovanovich.

[34] R Briffault, 1977, The Mothers, New York, Atheneum, p. 635.

[35] Frazer, op. cit., p. 243

[36] Davis, op. cit.
    J Needham, 1934, A History of Embryology, Cambridge, MA, Cambridge University Press.

[37] Briffault, op. cit., p. 252.

[38] Walker, op. cit., p.104

[39] Genesis, 4:16

[40] Thompson, 1981, op. cit., p. 163.

[41] T Jacobsen, 1976, The Treasures of Darkness: A History of Mesopotamian Religion, New Haven, CT, Yale University Press.
    SN Kramer, 1979, op. cit.
    D Wolkstein & S N Kramer, 1983, op. cit.

[42] Starhawk, 1989, <u>The Spiral Dance: A Rebirth of the Ancient Religion of the Great Goddess</u>, San Francisco, Harper.

[43] P Shuttle & P Redgrove, 1989, <u>The Wise Wound: Menstruation & Everywoman</u>, London, Paladin Books, pp. 197-224.

[44] H Kramer & J Sprenger, trans. 1928, <u>Malleus Malefi Carum</u>, Great Britain, John Rodher, pp. 54-66.

[45] J Highwater, 1990, <u>Myth and Sexuality</u>, Toronto, Canada, Penguin Books, p. 126.

[46] M Eliade, 1958, <u>Patterns in Comparative Religion</u>, New York, World Publishing, Meridian Books, pp. 261-2.

[47] Davis, op. cit., p. viii.

[48] JM Riddle, 1992, <u>Contraception and Abortion from the Ancient World to the Renaissance</u>, Cambridge, MA, Harvard University Press.

[49] Larousse, op. cit., p. 383.

[50] JE Blum, 1996, <u>Woman Heal Thyself: An Ancient Healing System for Contemporary Women</u>, Shaftesbury, Dorset, Great Britain: Element Books, p. 141. Kindly shown to me by Lisa Jackson.

[51] T Cleary, 1996, <u>Immortal Sisters: Secret Teachings of Taoist Women</u>, Berkeley, CA, North Atlantic Books, pp. 70-73.

[52] Blum, op. cit., p. 144.

[53] G Greer, 1985, <u>Sex and Destiny: The Politics of Human Fertility</u>, London, Picador, p. 130.

[54] E Neumann, 1991, <u>The Great Mother</u>, Princeton, NJ, Princeton University Press, p. 291.

[55] M Sjoo & B Mor, op. cit.
  L Shlain, 1998, <u>The Alphabet Versus the Goddess: The Conflict Between Word and Image</u>, New York, Viking Penguin.
  Stone, 1978, op. cit,
  Thompson, op. cit.

[56] J Achterberg, 1990, <u>Woman as Healer: A Panoramic Survey of the Healing Activities of Women from Prehistoric Times to the Present</u>, Boston, MA, Shambhala Publications.

[57] Shuttle& Redgrove, op. cit.

[58] A Diamant, 1998, <u>The Red Tent</u>, St Leonards, Australia, Allen & Unwin, p. 3

[59] Davis, op. cit., p. 56.

[60] M Woodman, 1993, Leaving My Father's House: A Journey to Conscious Femininity, London, Rider.

[61] P Kingsley, 1999, In the Dark Places of Wisdom, Inverness, Ca, The Golden Sufi Centre, p. 230.

[62] R Davies, 1992, The Cornish Trilogy: The Rebel Angels, What's Bred in the Bone, The Lyre of Orpheus, New York, Penguin.

[63] CG Jung, The dual mother, in Symbols of Transformation: An Analysis of the Prelude to a Case of Schizophrenia, CW 5, para. 589.

[64] E Gendlin, 1978, Focusing, New York, Everest House.

[65] D Feinstein & S Krippner, 1997, The Mythic Path: Discovering the Guiding Stories of Your Past - Creating a Vision for Your Future, New York, JP Tarcher.

[66] B Malinowski, 1929, The Sexual Life of Savages, New York, Harcourt, Brace, & World.

[67] ibid. p. 229.
After extensive research, Malinowski summarised the Islander's view of conception; a woman who is a virgin (nakapatu; na, female prefix; kapatu, closed, shut up) cannot give birth to a child, nor can she conceive, because nothing can enter or come out of her vulva. She must be opened up, or pierced through ... Thus the vagina of a woman who has much intercourse will be more open and easier for a spirit

child to enter. One that keeps fairly virtuous will have much poorer chances of becoming pregnant. But copulation is quite unnecessary except for its mechanical action.

[68] de Castillejo, op cit., p. 94.

[69] M Woodman, 1985, <u>The Pregnant Virgin: A Process of Psychological Transformation</u>, Toronto, Inner City Books, pp. 33-53.

[70] A Rosenblum, 1976, <u>The Natural Birth Control Book</u>, Philadelphia, PA, Aquarian Research Foundation.

[71] Private correspondence, 1993, Dr Vincent Priya, Malawi, Africa.

[72] B Malinowski, 1974, <u>Magic, Science and Religion and Other Essays</u>, Norwich, Great Britain, Fletcher & Son Ltd, p. 235.

[73] Davis, op. cit.

[74] G Lerner, 1986, <u>The Creation of Patriarchy</u>, New York, Oxford University Press, p. 151.

[75] D Lechniak, D Cieslak, & J Sosnowski, 1998, Morphology and developmental potential of bovine parthenotes after spontaneous activation in vitro, in <u>Journal of Applied Genetics, 39,</u> pp. 193-198.
    P Loi, S Ledda, J Fulka Jr, P Cappai, & RM Moor, 1998, Development of parthenogenetic and cloned ovine

embryos: effect of activation protocols, in <u>Biology of Reproduction, 58</u>, pp. 1177-1187.

S Nimura & T Asami, 1997, A histochemical study of the steroid metabolism in parthenogenetic mouse blastocysts, in <u>Journal of Reproduction and Development, 43</u>, pp. 251-256.

R Singh, MM Ahsan, & RK Datta, 1997, Artificial parthenogenesis in the silkworm Bombyx mori L., in <u>Indian Journal of Sericulture, 36</u>, pp. 87-91.

[76] B Spencer & FJ Gillen, 1904, <u>The Northern Tribes of Central Australia</u>, London, Macmillan & Co.

Spencer & Gillen began studying the Arunta people of Central Australia in 1896, before exposure to European settlers. Their report of initiation rites among the Arunta is hundreds of pages long and has been used as a reference for ancient practices which have seldom been observed in a relatively isolated culture.

Malinowski, 1974, op. cit., p. 232.

[77] R Lawlor, 1991, <u>Voices of the First day: Awakening the Aboriginal Dreamtime</u>, Vermont, VT: Inner Traditions International, Ltd., p.159.

There are stories of spontaneous abortion which suggest that many of the practices observed in pre-industrial cultures are about controlling rather than increasing fertility (see M Harris & E Ross, 1987, <u>Death, Sex, and Fertility</u>, New York, Columbia University Press.) This may have been especially prevalent among prehistoric foragers, where being able to control fertility in response to climate, food supply, mobility of the group, and other conditions may have ensured survival. Consistent with this, it was found that Aboriginal men do not consider children a means of perpetuating their individual achievements. Their understanding is that continued fertility has only become important in cultures where the emphasis is on owning land and overcoming nature to set up powerful agricultural settlements (Lawlor, p. 163). Observations of Aboriginal childbearing and rearing practices indicated that the low, stable Aboriginal population was due to the innate ability of the women to regulate conception and childbirth and avoid unnecessary birth, and that it is the patriarchal social order which has eroded this ability.

[78] D Abram, 1996, The spell of the Sensuous: Perception and Language in a More-Than-Human World, New York, Vintage Books, p. 167.

[79] M Mead, 1959, Male and Female: A Study of the Sexes in a Changing World, New York, Mentor Books, pp. 171-2.

[80] ibid. pp. 181-2.

[81] SW Tiffany & K Adams, 1985, The Wild Woman: An Inquiry into the Anthropology of an Idea, Vermont, VT, Schenkman Books, p. 18.

[82] B Bettelheim, 1955, Symbolic Wounds: Puberty Rites and the Envious Male, New York, Macmillan Collier, p. 20.

[83] K Horney, 1967, The flight from womanhood: The masculinity complex in women as viewed by men and by women, in H Kelman, ed., Feminine Psychology, New York, WW Norton, p. 61.

For further writings on the psychoanalytic study of male envy see also

E Fromm, 1951, The Forgotten Language, New York, Rinehart & Co.

E Jacobsen, 1950, The Psychoanalytic Study of the Child, New York, International University Press.

[84] 4. Spencer & Gillen, op. cit., p. 263.

The Australian Aboriginal practice of subincision is one example of a genital mutilation ritual. Subincision is a radical surgical procedure in which a cut is made in the ventral aspect of the penis; in many cases the incision is large enough to lay open most of the length of the penile urethra. The subincision wound was referred to by the same terms as those used to describe the vagina or womb, and the bleeding from the wound was equated with menstrual bleeding. This equating of bleeding from male genital mutilation with women's menstruation has also been observed in Wogeo and closely related Papuan cultures, where the bleeding was called 'men's menstruation' (I Hogbin, 1970, The Island of Menstruating Men: Religion in Wogeo, New Guinea, Scranton, PA, Chandler.)

Genital mutilation is at the core of the Aboriginal rite of the 'Kunapipi' which Bruno Bettleheim (op. cit. pp. 170-175) interpreted as a characteristic example of the ritualisation of men's desire to play a greater role in procreation. The word 'Kunapipi' apparently means both 'whistle-cock' (a subincision wound) and 'uterus of the mother'. The rites are based on the Kunapipi myth which tells of a great snake who is attracted to the female functions which involve blood. The essentially female sex functions of childbirth and menstruation arouse the snake which is attracted to the women and puts its head inside the hut in which they are hiding, and spouts forth a slippery substance, a saliva or semen. It can be interpreted that the symbolic intercourse of the snake entering the hut represents a means of acquiring or being a part of the female sex functions, especially as intercourse for the Aboriginal people is apparently not experienced primarily as an act of procreation, but may also be associated with merging psychologically and physically. In the myth, the three females are swallowed by the great snake, so that the stages of female development (child, pubescent girl, childbearing woman) are effectively acquired.

[85] KE Paige & JM Paige, (with L Fukler & E Magnus), 1981, The politics of reproductive ritual. Los Angeles, The University of California Press.

[86] Mead, op. cit., pp. 66-85.

[87] ibid. p. 78.

[88] JA Gupta, 1991, Women's bodies: The site for the ongoing conquest by reproductive technologies, in Issues in Reproductive and Genetic Engineering, 4, pp. 93-107.

See also R Rowland, 1992, Living Laboratories: Women and Reproductive Technologies, Sydney, Australia, Pan Macmillan.

[89] G Devereux, 1950, The psychology of feminine genital bleeding, in The International Journal of Psychoanalysis, XXXI, p. 252.

[90] MR Dexter, 1990, Whence the Goddesses: A Source Book, New York, Pergamon Press.
  P Weideger, 1976, Menstruation and Menopause, New York, Knopf.

[91] R Grimmassi, 2000, Italian Witchcraft: The Old religion of Southern Europe, St Paul, Minnesota, Llewellyn Publications, p. 197.

[92] de Castillejo, op. cit., p. 151.

[93] L. Kenton, 1995. Passage to Power: Natural Menopause Revolution. London, Random House, p 5.

[94] M Riley & J. Halliday, 2001. Births in Victoria 1999-2000. Victoria, Australia, Public Health Department of Human Services, p. 40.

[95] M Eliade, 1954, <u>The Myth of the Eternal Return</u>, Princeton, NJ, Princeton University Press.

See also CD Laughlin, J McManus, & EG d"Aquili, 1990, <u>Brain, Symbol & Experience:Toward a Neurophenomenology of Human Consciousness</u>, Boston, MA, New Science Library.

[96] AH Maslow, 1954, <u>Motivation and Personality</u>, New York, Harper & Row.

[97] ibid. p. 224.

[98] J Houston, 1987, <u>The Search for the Beloved: Journeys in Sacred Psychology</u>, Los Angeles, JP Tarcher, Inc.

[99] CG Jung, CW 1-18. CW - <u>The Collected Works of CG Jung</u>, 1953 - 1979, trans. RFC Hull, ed. H Read, M Fordham, G Adler, W McGuire, Bollingen Series XX, Princeton, NJ, Princeton University Press, vols. 1-18.

[100] E Neumann, 1991, <u>The Great Mother</u>, Princeton, NJ, Princeton University Press.

[101] CG Jung, 1964, <u>Man and His Symbols</u>, London, Aldus Books.

[102] CG Jung, The history and psychology of a natural symbol, in <u>Psychology and Religion: West and East</u>, CW 11, para. 165.

[103] J Hillman, 1992, <u>Revisioning Psychology</u>, New York, Harper Collins.

[104] CG Jung, On the nature of the psyche, in <u>The Structure and Dynamics of the Psyche</u>, CW 8, para. 420.

Jung explicitly addressed the integral connection of psyche and body, describing how spirit and matter meet in the psyche via archetypal and instinctual elements He described the "psychoid" aspect of the archetype as that which is "analogous to the position of physiological instinct, which is immediately rooted in the stuff of the organism and, with its psychoid nature, forms the bridge to matter in general".

[105] Phaedrus, trans. 1982.

[106] Jung, op. cit., CW 8.
This whole volume of the Collected Works is well worth reading as it contains many of the basic ingredients of Jung's understanding of the psyche.

[107] C Levi-Strauss, 1967, <u>Structural Anthropology</u>, Garden City, NY, Anchor.

Anthropologist, Claude Levi-Strauss, has identified 'unconscious infrastructures', the forms which emerge from collective experience.

N Tinbergen, 1951, <u>The Study of Instinct</u>, London, Oxford University Press.

Ethologist, Niko Tinbergen, described 'innate releasing mechanisms' (IRMs), structures in the central nervous system which are primed to activate when an appropriate stimulus is encountered in the environment.

[108] CG Jung, The Symbolic Life, CW 18, para. 1228.

[109] CG Jung, CW 8, op. cit.; The Archetypes of the Collective Unconscious, CW 9i.

G Adler, 1966, Studies in Analytical Psychology, New York, G. P. Putnam's Sons.

JA Hall, 1986, The Jungian Experience: Analysis and Individuation, Toronto, Canada, Inner City Books.

B Hannah, 1981, Encounters with the Soul: Active Imagination as Developed byC.G. Jung, Boston, Sigo Press.

Neumann, op. cit.

A Stevens, 1982, Archetype: A Natural History of the Self, London, Routledge & Kegan Paul.

----1997, The Two Million-Year-Old Self, New York, Fromm International.

EC Whitmont, 1991, The Symbolic Quest: Basic Concepts of Analytical Psychology, Princeton, NJ, Princeton University Press.

[110] Stevens, 1997, op. cit.; Whitmont, 1991, op. cit.

[111] CG Jung, 1971, Psychological Reflections: A New Anthology of his Writings 1905-1961, eds. J Jacobi & RFC Hull, Princeton, NJ, Princeton University Press, p. 76.

[112] Whitmont, 1982, op. cit., p. vii.

[113] Starhawk, 1989, <u>The Spiral Dance: A Rebirth of the Ancient Religion of the Great Goddess</u>. San   Francisco, Harper.

[114] BG Walker, 1990, <u>Women's Rituals: A Source Book</u>, San Francisco, Harper & Row, p. xvii.

[115] Eisler, 1988, op. cit., p. xvii. See http://www.rianeeisler.com/ for the important work Riane Eisler is doing in the world today.

[116] ibid. p. 194.

[117] CG Jung, 1974, <u>Dreams</u>, trans. RFC Hull, Princeton, Princeton University Press, p. 241.

[118] Wolkstein & Kramer, op. cit.

[119] See the article on " The 'Queen of the Night' relief, Old Babylonian, 1800-1750 BC, Iraq" on the British Museum website, http://www.britishmuseum.org/explore/highlights/highlight_objects/me/t/queen_of_the_night_relief.aspx

[120] Thompson, op. cit., p. 17.

[121] B D Meador, 1992, <u>Uncursing the Dark: treasures From the Underworld</u>, Wilmette, IL, Chiron Publications, pp. 126-7.

[122] C G Jung, Analytical psychology and education, in The Development of Personality. Papers on Child Psychology, Education, and Related Subjects, CW 17, para. 219n.

[123] C Zweig, 1990, To Be a Woman: The Birth of the Conscious Feminine, Los Angeles, Jeremy T Tarcher Inc.

[124] As well as the books already listed in the text, the following specifically address the emergence of the feminine principle into contemporary experience.

JS Bolen, 1984, Goddesses in Everywoman: A New Psychology of Women San Francisco, Harper & Row.
EW Gadon, 1989, The Once and Future Goddess: A Symbol for Our Time, New York, Harper & Row.
RA Johnson, 1989, She: Understanding Feminine Psychology, New York, Harper & Row.
EC Whitmont, 1982, Return of the Goddess, Guernsey, Channel Islands, Great Britain, The Guernsey Press Co., Ltd.

It may well be that in exploring the feminine principle, psychological research can re-engage the meaning and depth of psyche as an embodied experience, promoting greater involvement with the everyday experience of the world rather than designing the definitive experiment, or refining tools of measurement and analysis.

[125] Whitmont, 1982, op. cit. p. vii.

[126] M Gimbutas, 1989, The Language of the Goddess, New York, Harper & Row.

[127] T Lee, 1989, Women as Demons: The Male Perception of Women Through Time and Space, London, The Women's Press Ltd, p. ix.
[128] T Robbins, 1984 , Jitterbug Perfume, New York, Bantam Books, p. 56.

[129] Neumann, op. cit.

[130] Gimbutas, 1989, op. cit., p. 316.

Amongst others, Gimbutas points out that Neumann's description of the Great Mother was based on historical material that reflected the takeover of the Goddess religions by ideologies which consistently degraded and distorted the feminine. So many of the myths and stories which have come to us suffer from this distortion. I have, however, found that the profound study of the feminine principle in Jungian psychology does offer a basis for describing otherwise invisible, unknowable processes of the human psyche and offer a map for the journey. Even while the ancient Greek myths often refer to the Goddesses in terms of their relationship with the masculine, they nevertheless introduce us to the archetypal feminine and invite a closer look.

This criticism has, also been extended to Jungian psychology more generally (Sjoo & Mor, op. cit.). The main reservation I have with Neumann's work in this area arises from the assumption of a hierarchical structure of consciousness, with the implication that the elementary character is lower on the developmental scale than the transformative. I prefer to understand the two as descriptions of different forms of consciousness, both serving a vital function in the human experience for males and females alike.

[131] Neumann, op. cit., p. 25.

[132] JO Stevens, 1971, <u>Awareness: Exploring Experimenting Experiencing</u>, Moab, UT, Real People Press, p. 40.

This method of conscious identification is similar to the Buddhist idea that full concentration and meditation on anything can lead to full knowing and understanding of human experience (see T Nhat Hanh, 1987, <u>The Miracle of Mindfulness: A Manual on Meditation</u>, Boston, MA, Beacon Press.)

[133] The idea of internal dialogue is an inherent part of analytical psychology and has been developed into various therapeutic approaches.

See CG Jung, CW 8, op. cit., para. 185-189;

R Assagioli, 1973, <u>The Act of Will</u>, Baltimore, Penguin;

F Perls, R Hefferline, & P Goodman, 1951, <u>Gestalt Therapy</u>, New York, Bantam.

[134] Whitmont, 1982, op. cit., p. 78.

[135] Neumann, op. cit., p. 58.

[136] ibid. p. 50.

[137] G Lakoff & M Johnson, 1981, The metaphorical structure of the human conceptual system, in DA Norman, ed., Perspectives on Cognitive Science. First Annual Meeting of the Cognitive Science Society, Logola, CA, Ablex Publishing Corp., pp. 74-75.

[138] Woodman, 1993, op.cit., p. 1.

[139] Woodman, 1993, op. cit., p. 7.

[140] S de Beauvoir, 1952, The Second Sex, New York, Bantam Books, p. 71.

[141] E Jong, 1979, Creativity vs generativity: The unexplained lie, in New Republic Jan. 13, p. 27.

[142] de Beauvoir, op. cit., p. 467.

[143] E Martin, 1987, The Woman in the Body: A Cultural Analysis of Reproduction, Boston, Beacon Press, p. 157.

[144] D Meltzer, 1981, Birth: An Anthology of Ancient Texts, Songs, Prayers, and Stories, San Francisco, North Point Press.

[145] Jung, CW 8, op. cit., para. 135.

[146] J Achterberg, 1985, <u>Imagery in Healing: Shamanism and Modern Medicine</u>, Boston, MA, Shambhala Publications.

[147] J Hailfax, 1982, <u>Shaman: The Wounded Healer</u>, London, Thames and Hudson.

[148] Achterberg, 1985, op. cit.
N Cousins, 1983, <u>The Healing Heart</u>, New York, WW Norton.
D Zwar, 1985, <u>Doctor Ahead of His Time: The Life of Psychiatrist Dr Ainslie Meares</u>,
Richmond, Australia, Greenhouse Publications.

[149] Bruner, op. cit., p. 12.

[150] S Wolinsky, 1991, <u>Trances People Live: Healing Approaches in Quantum Psychology</u>, Falls Village, CT, The Bramble Company

[151] Pert, op. cit., p. 258.

[152] N Ellis, 1988, <u>Awakening Osiris: A New Translation of The Egyptian Book of the Dead</u>, Grand Rapids, MI, Phanes Press, p. 122.

[153] M Merleau-Ponty, 1962, <u>Phenomenology of Perception</u>, trans. C.Smith, London, Routledge & Kegan Paul, p. 212.

See also
----1964, <u>The Primacy of Perception</u>, Evanstion, IL, Northwestern University Press.

----1968, <u>The Visible and the Invisible</u>, Evanston, IL, Northwestern University Press.

[154] Boston Women's health Book Collective, 1996, <u>The New Our Bodies, Ourselves</u>, eds. A Phillips & J Rakusen, New York, Penguin Books, especially Chapter 3, The anatomy and physiology of sexuality and reproduction, pp. 29-41.

L Nilsson, 1990, <u>A Child is Born</u>, New York, Bantam Doubleday Dell.
Clear photographs and diagrams of female and male reproductive organs and the process of conception. Useful to develop imagery of the internal body processes involved in conception.

NB Payne & BL Richardson, 1997, <u>The Language of fertility: A revolutionary Mind-Body program for Conscious Conception</u>, New York, Harmony Books.
Although this book approaches the mindbody connection from the perspective of making babies rather than preventing conception, it does support the reality of mindbody fertility management.

[155] K Bowers, 1977, Hypnosis: An informational approach, in <u>Annuals of the New York Academy of Sciences, 296,</u> 222-237, p. 231

[156] H Selye, 1936\1976, <u>The Stress of Life</u>, New York, McGraw-Hill.

[157] G Harris, 1948, Steps toward a cell-biological alphabet for elementary forms of learning, in G Lynch, J McGaugh & N Weinberger, eds. Neurobiology of Learning and Memory, New York, Guilford Press.

E Scharrer & B Scharrer, 1940, Secretory Cells Within the Hypothalamus.Research Publications of the Association of Nervous and Mental Diseases, New York, Hafner

[158] Pert, op. cit.

[159] EL Rossi, 1988, The Psychobiology of Mind-Body Healing: New Concepts of Therapeutic Hypnosis, New York, WW Norton.

[160] J Stewart, W Krebs, & E Kaczender, 1971, State-dependent learning produced with steroids, Nature, 216, pp. 1233-1234.

[161] J Blankstein, F Reyes, J Winter, & C Faiman, 1981, Endorphins and the regulation of the human menstrual cycle, Clinical Endocrinology, 14, (3), pp. 287-294

[162] WF Crowley, RW Whitcomb, JL Jameson, J Weiss, JS Finkelstein, & LSL O'Dea, 1991, Neuroendocrine control of human reproduction in the male, in Recent Progress in Hormone Research, 47, pp. 27-67.

Specific research into the neuroendocrine control of human reproduction is a relatively recent area of study. Previously this was hampered by obstacles to the study of gonadotropin-releasing hormone (GnRH), a hypothalamic hormone which controls the synthesis and secretion of the pituitary gonadotropin hormones, LH and FSH, the hormones involved in the menstrual cycle. It was initially found that the rapid metabolism of GnRH made its direct measurement in the peripheral circulation limited in its usefulness in defining the neuroendocrine control of human reproduction (DJ Handelsman, RPS Jansen, LM Boylan, JA Spaliviero,& JR Turtle, 1984, Pharmacokinetics of gonadotropin-releasing hormone: comparison of subcutaneous and Intravenous routes, in Journal of Clinical Endocrinology and Metabolism, 59, pp. 739-746).

Measurement was also complicated by the relative inaccessibility of the blood supply close to the point of secretion. This means that accurate measurement would be technically difficult and personally intrusive. Based on the experimental evidence from several species that release of LH from the anterior pituitary reflects secretion of GnRH by the hypothalamus, the indirect measurement of GnRH secretion has become increasingly accessible resulting in a clearer understanding of the role of the hypothalamus in the neuroendocrine regulation of gonadotropin secretion in the human

See:
IJ Clarke & JT Cummins, 1982, The temporal relationship between Gonadotropin-releasing hormone and luteinizing hormone secretion in ovariectomized ewes, in Endocrinology, 111, p. 1737.

FJ Hayes & WF Crowley Jr, 1998, Gonadotropin pulsations across development, in Hormone Research, 49, pp. 163-168.

FJ Karsch, EL Bittman, DL Foster, RL Goodman, SJ Legan, & JE Robinson, 1984, Neuroendocrine basis of seasonal reproduction, in Recent Progress in Hormone Research, 40, pp.185-232.

JE Levine, KYF Pau, VD Ramirez, & GL Jackson, 1982, Simultaneous measurement of Luteinizing hormone releasing hormone and luteinizing hormone release in unanaesthetized ovariectomized sheep, IN Endocrinology, 111, pp. 1449-1455.

DI Spratt, WF Crowley, JP Butler, AR Hoffman, PM Conn, & TM Badger, 1985, Pituitary luteinizing hormone responses to intravenous and subcutaneous administration of gonadotropin-releasing hormone in men, in Journal of Clinical Endocrinology and Metabolism, 61, pp. 890-895.

[163] JC Marshall, AC Dalkin, DJ Haislender, SJ Paul, GA Ortolano, & RP Kelch, 1991, Gonadotropin-releasing hormone pulses: Regulators of gonadotropin synthesis and ovulatory cycles, in Recent Progress in Hormone Research, 47, pp. 155-187.

[164] N Groome, PJ Illingworth, M O"Brien, I Cooke, TS Ganesan, DT Baird, & AS McNeilly, 1994, Detection of

dimesic inhibin throughout the human menstrual cycle, in Clinical Endocrinology, 40, pp. 717-723.

[165] DB Seifer & G Lambert-Messerlian, 1997, Predictive value of serum inhibin-B for ART outcome?, in Fertility and Sterility, 68, pp.947-948.

[166] RE Leach, KS Moghissi, JF Randolph, NE Reame, CM Blacker, KA Ginsburg, & MP Diamond, 1997, Intensive hormone monitoring in women with unexplained infertility: Evidence for subtle abnormalities suggestive of diminished ovarian reserve, in Fertility and Sterility, 68, pp. 413-420.

[167] H Crasilneck & J Hall, 1984, Clinical Hypnosis, New York, Grune & Stratton.
MH Erickson, 1960, Psychogenic alteration of menstrual functioning: Three instances, in The American Journal of Clinical Hypnosis, 2, pp. 227-231.

[168] J Achterberg, 1985, Imagery in Healing: Shamanism and Modern Medicine, Boston, MA, Shambala Publications, Inc.
R Ader, D Felton, & N Cohen, 1991, Psychoneuroimmunology, San Diego, CA, Academic Press.
Pert, op.cit.

[169] Achterberg, 1985, op. cit., p. 199.

[170] R Guillemin, 1978, Peptides in the brain: The new endocrinology of the neuron, in Science, 202, pp. 390-402.

J Henry, 1982, Circulating opioids: Possible physiological roles in central nervous function, in Neuroscience & Biobehavioural Reviews, 6, pp. 229-245.

 S Snyder, 1980, Brain peptides as neurotransmitters, in Science, 209, pp. 976-983.

[171] J Davis, 1984, Endorphins, New York, Dial Press.

[172] Pert, op. cit.

[173] ibid. p. 23.

[174] Rossi, op. cit., p. 203.

[175] Gupta, op. cit.

 JG Raymond, 1995, Women as Wombs: Reproductive Technologies and the Battle Over Women's Freedom, North Melbourne, Australia, Spinifex Press.

 Rowland, op. cit.

[176] J Achterberg, B Dossey, & L Kolkmeier, 1994, Rituals of Healing: Using Your Imagination for Health and Wellness, New York, Bantam Books.

[177] The Sheela na Gig project www.sheelanagig.org. The (in)famous Kilpeck Sheela Na Gig, 2006-02-25 (original upload date). Originally from en.wikipedia.

Released under the GNU Free Documentation License
[178] M E Harding, 1973. Psychic Energy: Its Source and its Transformation. Princeton, NJ: Princeton University Press. p 126.

[179] CG Jung, 1990. The Mother Archetype in Archetype and the Collective Unconscious, CW Vol 9, Part 1. Para 156. Princeton, NJ: Princeton University Press.

[180] Ibid.

[181] N Frye, 1982. The Great Code: The Bible and Literature. New York, Harcourt Brace Jovanovich, p. xviii.

[182] EC Whitmont, 1982. Return of the Goddess, Guernsey, GB, The Guernsey Press. p. vii.

[183] CG Jung (1973). Psychological Reflections: A New Anthoology of His Writings. RFC Hull & J Jacobi, Eds. Princeton University Press, p. 14.

[184] Ibid., p. 153.

[185] "A Private Universe" was created and produced by Matthew H. Schneps and Philip M. Sadler, Harvard Smithsonian Center for Astrophysics. Partial funding for "A Private Universe" was provided by the National Science Foundation. http://www.learner.org/teacherslab/pup/ URL accessed 10/5/06.

[186] E H Schein (2002-4) Kurt Lewin's Change Theory in the Field and in the Classroom: Notes Toward a Model of Managed Learning

http://www.a2zpsychology.com/ARTICLES/kurt_lewin's_change_theory_page7.htm

[187] CG Jung, 1990. The Archetypes of the Collective Unconscious. Translated by RFC Hull. Bollingen Series XX. The Collected Works of CG Jung, Vol 9, part 1, para 67.

[188] J Achterberg, 1985. Imagery in Healing: Shamanism and Modern Medicine. Boston, MA: Shambhala Publications

[189] B Trubshaw, 1995. The metaphors and rituals of place and time - an introduction to liminality or Why Christopher Robin wouldn't walk on the cracks. Mercian Mysteries, No.22, February. http://www.indigogroup.co.uk/edge/liminal.htm

[190] The Australian Concise Oxford Dictionary of Current English. 1987. Melbourne: Oxford University Press. p. 353.

[191] Ibid., p. 1207.

[193] C G Jung, CW - The Collected Works of CG Jung, 1953-1979, trans. RFC Hull, ed. H Read, M Fordham, G Adler, W McGuire, Bollingen Series XX. Princeton, NJ, Princeton University Press, vols. 1-17.

[194] C B Pert, 1997. Molecules of Emotion: Why You Feel the Way You Feel. New York, Scribner.

[195] G Bateson, 1978a. The pattern which connects. Coevolution Quarterly, 18, pp. 4-15.

[196] G Edelman, 1987. Neural Darwinism: The Theory of Neuronal Group Selection. New York, Basic Books.

----1989. The Remembered Present: A Biological Theory of Consciousness. New York, Basic Books.

----1992. Bright Air, Brilliant Fire: On the Matter of Mind. New York, Basic Books.

[197] G Bateson, 1981. Paradigmatic conservatism, in G Wider-Mott & JH Weakland, eds.,

Rigor and Imagination: Essays from the Legacy of Gregory Bateson. New York, Praeger Publishers, p. 43.